Humanity Over Comfort

This book is authored by six unapologetic Black women, so we dedicate this book to six unapologetic Black women ancestors—Audre, Doris, Harriett, Louella, Mary, and Vernelle.

*Because of you, we **can**, we **are**, and we **will**.*

Humanity Over Comfort

How You Confront Systemic Racism Head On

Sharone Brinkley-Parker

Tracey L. Durant

Kendra V. Johnson

Kandice Taylor

Johari Toe

Lisa Williams

FOR INFORMATION:

Corwin

A SAGE Company

2455 Teller Road

Thousand Oaks, California 91320

(800) 233-9936

www.corwin.com

SAGE Publications Ltd.

1 Oliver's Yard

55 City Road

London, EC1Y 1SP

United Kingdom

SAGE Publications India Pvt. Ltd.

B 1/I 1 Mohan Cooperative Industrial Area

Mathura Road, New Delhi 110 044

India

SAGE Publications Asia-Pacific Pte. Ltd.

18 Cross Street #10-10/11/12

China Square Central

Singapore 048423

President: Mike Soules

Associate Vice President and
    Editorial Director: Monica Eckman

Acquisitions Editor: Dan Alpert

Senior Content Development Editor: Lucas Schleicher

Associate Content Development Editor: Mia Rodriguez

Production Editor: Megha Negi

Copy Editor: Colleen Brennan

Typesetter: Hurix Digital

Proofreader: Jeff Bryant

Cover Designer: Janet Kiesel

Marketing Manager: Sharon Pendergast

Library of Congress Cataloging-in-Publication Data

Names: Brinkley-Parker, Sharone, author. | Durant, Tracey L., author. | Johnson, Kendra, V., author. | Taylor, Kandice, author. | Toe, Johari, author. | Williams, Lisa, author.

Title: Humanity over comfort : how you confront systemic racism head on / Sharone Brinkley-Parker, Tracey L. Durant, Kendra V. Johnson, Kandice Taylor, Johari Toe, Lisa Williams.

Description: Thousand Oaks, California : Corwin, a SAGE company, [2022] | Includes bibliographical references and index.

Identifiers: LCCN 2021024611 | ISBN 9781071847916 (paperback) | ISBN 9781071847923 (epub) | ISBN 9781071847930 (epub) | ISBN 9781071847947 (ebook)

Subjects: LCSH: Racism in education–United States. | Educational equalization–United States. | Anti-racism–United States.

Classification: LCC LC212.2 .B75 2022 | DDC 371.82996073–dc23

LC record available at https://lccn.loc.gov/2021024611

This book is printed on acid-free paper.

21 22 23 24 25 10 9 8 7 6 5 4 3 2 1

Contents

Acknowledgments   vii

About the Authors   ix

How to Use This Book   1

Part I: Beginning the Journey - The Reflecting Space

Chapter 1: Race Matters Because Racism Does   9

Chapter 2: Building Community by
Reimagining New Possibilities   25

Chapter 3: Confronting Blame by
Reframing Accountability   35

Part II: Leaning Into the Learning - The Making
Meaning Space

Chapter 4: Power and Influence   55

Chapter 5: Invisibility and Other Barriers
to Engaging in the Work of Anti-Racism
and Structural Transformation   71

Part III: Curating Transformation - The Doing Space

Chapter 6: Creating Space for Productive Struggle   87

Chapter 7: Application of Equity Lens
for System Change   97

Chapter 8: Building to Transformation
Through Collective Application   113

Chapter 9: Final Thoughts   125

References   **131**

Index   **139**

Acknowledgments

We, six Black women, wrote this book in a moment in our collective history when Black men and women—trans, gay, queer, cis, and non-binary—have been subjected to tremendous racialized stress and trauma. As we wrote this book, America in general, Black America in particular, held its breath at the possibility that the murder of George Floyd might go without accountability. What would a decision that did not assign culpability mean for Black people, for Brown people, for all people? Where would we go from such a decision? Luckily, that question did not need exploration because responsibility was assigned. But, we submit, in acknowledgment of this work, that the larger question of where we go from here is yet unanswered. It is not a simple question. It indeed has generational reach . . . from the past into the future. This is what we want to acknowledge. We stand in the long shadow of the bravery and wisdom of the ancestors, that they survived, that they challenged us to thrive, so we can challenge you to thrive. This book is our effort to bear witness to what it does not have to be. Marginalization, exclusion, and minimization are an affront to humanity. To change these things, we must change ourselves. Upon being changed, we might collectively change systems and structures that perpetuate inhumanity.

So, it is with a deep and abiding love of humanity that we offer you our words filled with joy, pain, possibility, curiosity, and hope.

Further, it is with love and appreciation that we extend gratitude to three dynamic Black women—Drs. Kelly Mack, Penelope Martin-Knox, and Wendy Shaia—for taking time out of their valuable schedules to offer a peer review of this book. We honor their time, insight, and authentic investment in our contribution to the restoration of our collective humanity!

About the Authors

Dr. Sharone Brinkley-Parker

Dr. Sharone Brinkley-Parker has presented on topics of leadership, curriculum and standards, and equity and access in education while consulting with several entities. She has facilitated sessions in conjunction with Maryland Cultural Proficiency Conference, National Alliance for Partnerships in Equity (NAPE), Maryland Multicultural Coalition Conference, and UnboundEd. While facilitating sessions and providing development, she has supported the expansion of educators, leaders, and educational internal and external stakeholders in the areas of standards-aligned instruction, strategic leadership, culturally responsive instruction, and cultural proficiency.

Dr. Brinkley-Parker is a native of Baltimore, Maryland. She was educated in the public school system and has earned degrees from Morgan State (B.S. in health education; Ed.D. in urban educational leadership with a concentration in social policy) and Towson (M.A.T) universities. Her dissertation study examined the lived experience of suspension on African American male students. She has more than 20 years' experience as an educator, where she has served as a teacher of middle school ELA, math, social studies, and writing and of high school algebra. She has also been a grant writer, MESA coordinator, grade-level chair, assistant principal, principal, and district-level administrator with two separate school systems within the state of Maryland.

Dr. Brinkley-Parker is one of six founding members of Greater Baltimore Health Improvement Initiative, a community-based group seeking to empower communities within Baltimore City around health responsibility through education, advocacy, and action. Additionally, she is a proud member of Alpha Kappa Alpha Sorority, Inc.

She is also a founding partner in Equity in Education Partners, an organization that works to dismantle structural and systemic racism, sexism, classism, and ableism to ensure access for multi-racial/multi-ethnic communities. Dr. Brinkley-Parker is the proud mom of two beautiful daughters, Sage and Sijya, and SheeShee to the amazing Karter. The passion she exudes as a result of experiencing motherhood drives her passion for facilitating equity work to ensure all students have equitable access throughout their educational career; this is what compels us to make the invisible visible and champion for the voiceless.

Dr. Tracey L. Durant

Dr. Tracey Lynette Durant has over 20 years of experience in the educational and non-profit fields having worked as a specialist, director, executive director, program administrator, and learning assistance coordinator. She has most recently held roles where she has been responsible for leading systemwide initiatives designed to promote the utilization of equitable practices, systems, and structures that ensure positive educational outcomes for students. A graduate of Western Senior High School, Dr. Durant holds degrees from Sojourner-Douglass College, Coppin State University, and Morgan State University.

Dr. Durant is a founding partner with Equity in Education Partners, focused on capacity building to dismantle systems of oppression that operate in social services organizations. She is an equity instructor with the National Alliance for Partnerships in Equity providing professional development focused on improving underserved populations' access to and success in educational and training programs that lead to high-skill, high-wage, and high-demand careers. She is also a licensed consultant with the Standards for Excellence Institute where she provides coaching and support to non-profit organizations in the State of Maryland.

Some of her accomplishments include being selected as the Millers-Coors/100 Black Men of America Ice Cold Leader, named one of the Daily Record's Top 100 Women and a Leading Woman,

Sojourner-Douglass College Distinguished Alum, and the inaugural recipient of the CollegeBound Foundation Distinguished Alumni Award. Dr. Durant's current professional and community service activities include board chair, Child First Authority; board chair, Chimes Foundation, Inc.; president, Maryland Multicultural Coalition; advisory board member, Positive Schools Center; and member of Delta Sigma Theta Sorority, Inc. She is married to Bruce Jr. and the proud mother of Cheyenne and Bruce III.

Dr. Kendra V. Johnson

Dr. Kendra V. Johnson's preferred pronouns are "she" and "her." She holds a bachelor's degree in chemistry from Lincoln University, PA. While working the in the field of education, Dr. Johnson went on to earn her master's degree in administration and supervision from Johns Hopkins University, a juris doctorate with concentrations in public interest and business law from the University of Baltimore School of Law, and a doctorate in urban educational leadership, social policy from Morgan State University. Dr. Johnson is licensed to practice law in the states of Maryland and New Jersey. Accordingly, Dr. Johnson comes to this work with rich and dynamic experiences in education and law. Before serving as a community superintendent, she served as a science teacher, science department chairperson, assistant principal, assistant to the area superintendent, principal, area assistant superintendent, Title I coordinator, instructional director, assistant superintendent, a chief academic and innovation officer, an assistant superintendent for equity, and superintendent.

Dr. Johnson brings experiences from multiple educational settings over the past 25 years: large, mid-size, and small districts; urban and suburban districts; and racially, socio-economically, and linguistically diverse districts. Dr. Johnson draws from these authentic experiences to inform her work with students, parents/guardians, educators, and community members. In particular, she honors the voice of children, and believes their voice should serve as "the expert voice" when attempting to effectively program for them. Dr. Johnson and co-author Dr. Lisa Williams wrote the book, *When Treating All the Kids the Same Is the Real Problem* (Corwin, 2014). This book and related leadership, equity, social justice, access, and opportunity topics serve as the content for

Dr. Johnson's consulting and executive coaching with non-profit organizations, public schools, and private/independent schools. Dr. Johnson's commitment to dismantle systems of oppression and actively advance social justice continues to evolve through her experiences as an educator, pro bono attorney, consultant, unapologetic "let's be who we say we are" advocate, member of the illustrious sisterhood of Delta Sigma Theta Sorority, Inc., and founding partner with Equity in Education Partners. She resides in the Baltimore area with her partner, Reginald.

Dr. Kandice Taylor

Dr. Kandice Taylor is a goal-driven experienced school administrator who has achieved success and recognition for improving student outcomes in schools identified as "challenging." She demonstrates skills in analyzing issues, improving student achievement outcomes, building community among staff to change the climate and culture of the school environment, and building capacity in teacher leaders. Dr. Taylor has received state-level citations for her school transformation efforts and county-level honors, including the 2018–2019 Secondary Principal of the Year award.

Dr. Taylor has over 20 years of active leadership experience in public and higher education with the past 10 years focused on transformational leadership while building capacity among aspiring leaders. She has served as a teacher, an assistant principal, an assistant to the assistant superintendent, and a principal. Dr. Taylor also works as a lecturer and mentor principal for graduate students at Morgan State University and has served as a consulting principal for Towson University. She is also a founding partner in Equity in Education Partners, an organization that works to dismantle structural and systemic racism, sexism, classism, and ableism to ensure access for multi-racial/multi-ethnic communities.

Dr. Taylor received a B.S. in telecommunications from Morgan State University, an M.A. in leadership in teaching and English from Notre Dame of Maryland University, and an Ed.D. in urban education with a social policy concentration from Morgan State University.

Ms. Johari Toe

Ms. Johari Toe is a public school administrator who is an advocate for all students, parents, teachers, and stakeholders. Ms. Toe is dedicated to creating a purposeful, equitable, rigorous, and engaging learning environment for all children. She was educated in the Baltimore City Public Schools and upon completion of high school, she enrolled in college. Ms. Toe holds a bachelor's degree from Morgan State University and a master's degree from Towson University.

Ms. Toe has over 20 years of experience in the field of education. She has been a classroom teacher at the middle school level, instructional coach, professional developer, Title I specialist, assistant principal, and principal in various school systems in the state of Maryland. In addition to her professional experiences, she has worked with multiple non-profit organizations and is a current board member with the Child First Authority. Ms. Toe has invested in the theory and practice of how to create equitable work environments though the avenue of professional development. Some of the topics cover studying and presenting professional developments to diverse audiences, discussing equity and education, Doors Wide Shut: Strategies to Identify Deficits in Parent Involvement, Transitioning From Voice to Action: Strategies to Improve Parent Involvement, Using Climate Data to Discover Hidden Voices, Social Workers: A Key Element in Building Successful Inclusive School Communities, and There Is Power in Focusing on Student Groups.

Dr. Lisa Williams

Dr. Lisa Williams is a career educator, having held the position of teacher, mentor, university professor, and Title I director, and executive director of equity over her career in education. She has bachelors' degrees in biology and psychology, an M.S. in psychology, and a doctorate in Urban Educational Leadership with an emphasis in social policy. She has presented at the local, state, and national levels on topics related to improving outcomes for marginalized student populations.

Her career in public education spans nearly 20 years. Her dissertation study examined Response to Intervention (RTI) and the performance of students attending Title I schools.

Dr. Williams is a consultant with the National Alliance for Partnerships in Equity (NAPE) as well as her independent company, EMCS. In her consulting work, she has provided guidance for schools and school systems in the areas of anti-racist organizational development, racial equity, gender equity in STEM, leading for equity, school transformation, and culturally responsive practices. Dr. Williams has served as a subject matter expert with the U.S. Department of Education Department of Career, Technical, and Adult Education division related to equitable access in STEM/CTE. She serves as a board president for Restorative Response Baltimore, an organization that provides guidance and support for Restorative Practices and Community Conferences to decrease violence and create inclusive environments across the Baltimore Metropolitan Area.

Over her career as a public school educator and administrator, systems transformation toward equitable access has been her focus. Toward that end, she has engaged in program creation (created two certificate programs in educational equity and cultural proficiency with two local Maryland Institutes for Higher Education) that help build staff capacity to actualize inclusive schooling behaviors. Her first book, *When Treating All the Kids the Same Is the Real Problem* (co-authored with Dr. Kendra Johnson), was published by Corwin in 2014. Dr. Williams is the proud mom of a son, Andrew, who is the daily inspiration for her work for all children.

How to Use This Book

This book is intended to help readers develop their ability to engage in both capacity building and leadership practices that dismantle systems of oppression. The authors advance ideas, ways of being, and practices to address not only the straightforward aspects of this work but also the nuances. This textured exploration is needed because systems of advantages and disadvantages live in society as natural and normal. In order to actualize organizational transformation and dislodge systems of oppression, we must begin to interrogate the very idea of what is "natural" and "normal." To serve this overarching goal, the authors want you to *feel something*. We want you to diversify the ways you understand how marginalization occurs. The journey to understanding race as it intersects with other marginalized identities in America is a labor of both the head and the heart. The authors would offer that your full self-engagement is your best self-engagement. When you show up as your best engaged self, the fullness of your humanity is also present. The authors intentionally use language that the authors believe will elicit an emotional response from readers, including the potential feeling of discomfort. The authors do so to challenge and reframe the reader's current understanding and application of intersectional issues of racial equality and social justice.

The authors also believe that this learning journey is deeply personal. For this reason, the authors have included a variety of tools to contextualize the work so individuals and/or organizations might find their appropriate entry point and personalized developmental pathway. The reality, however, is that many may simply need to start at the beginning. The beginning for many is to uncover the stories they have been told and interrogate how these stories position them to function in their lives, the family, community, and organization. Based on what individuals, teams, and groups come to understand through this process, how do they "relearn" what they think about how America got to this point? But most importantly, what will they determine needs to be done to center, value, and honor the humanity of the collective? We know that the past cannot be changed, but what we understand about the past can serve to bolster resolve in the kind of present and future that we collectively elect to create.

American history is rich, dynamic, sad, horrific, powerful, and disturbing all at the same time. Being a great America is not in conflict with being a complex America. Being a great America without being a complex, often inconsistent, America is not possible. We want to decouple worthiness from the need to valorize history. Our challenge, in this moment, is that some believe we cannot honor our greatness as a people and a nation if we openly discuss our complex history. Not only is this belief false, but it is dangerous if we ever intend to live up to the great ideas this nation purports as fundamental to its existence.

The authors are proud Americans, so this internal realization of our dark and complex history is one the authors bear with readers. To help readers along the way, the authors created the following chart to describe the features and tools that run throughout the book. The content will inform when authors elect to utilize these tools.

THROUGHOUT THE BOOK		
Tool	**Purpose**	**Intended Reaction(s)**
Chapter Reflection	To call the reader's attention to examples from the book that requires reflection or pause	To connect the learning to readers' personal experiences and/or highlight nuances that readers may have noticed in their learning/lived experiences to date
Journal Prompts	To provide additional opportunities for readers to pause and offer personal responses as they make meaning of the text	
Pause and Reflect, Ideas to Sit With, and Interruptions	To promote reader reflection as readers interact with text as well as to highlight essential points—whether to challenge the reader's understanding of where dominance might exist and where transformation is needed or simply stop and chew on content more deeply	
Scenarios	To provide a lived experience to situate the learning	
What Nobody Talks About	To call forward the nuances that require responses that we tend to undervalue and/or not discuss	
Your Lived Experience	To ask readers to use their sphere of influence as they center and situate the new learning directly in their own lives	

Equally as important, the authors offer a few definitions of concepts and ideas to norm readers with our thinking. The concepts and ideas include but are not limited to the following.

Anti-Oppression: An idea that advances, in principle and practice, the equal treatment of identity. A lens of anti-oppression guides its users to consider the intersected, interlocking systems of marginalizing practices that compound to reproduce predictable advantage and disadvantage in service of disrupting said practices and replacing them with those that are equally accessible.

Anti-Racism: An active process of disrupting the conceptual and material manifestation of patterns that advantage Whiteness (inclusive of Eurocentric culture and people called White) over all others. The authors contend that anti-racism involves more than simply opposing racist ideas and policies. To be an anti-racist, you must actively challenge the reproduction of racialized outcomes. There is a certain level of consciousness that must be acquired to engage in anti-racist work. When individuals declare themselves as anti-racists without the consciousness of their actions, these individuals are usually supporting racist systems and showing up as performative.

Equity: Unlike equality, equity is the idea of giving individuals what they need to survive and succeed. Equity takes into account the effects of discrimination and aims for a just outcome.

Humanity: The notion of showing a compassionate, sympathetic, and generous behavior or disposition for each human irrespective of gender, class, ability (physical and mental), ethnicity, native language, or other aspects of identity.

Institutional Racism: Closely connected to systemic racism but different. Remember those beliefs that still lingered after laws were abolished and/or statutes amended? Today the beliefs are still dwelling and operating under the veil in many institutions (e.g., preK–12 institutions or local police departments). Irrespective of changes in laws and/or policies, there are traditions, beliefs, opinions, and even myths that are crystalized into the fiber of institutions. Institutions seeking to examine how racism and other forms of marginalization might be operating can start by examining data to assess patterns of predictability.

Intersectional Racial Equity: A lens of analysis that centers race as it interfaces with other aspects of identity such as gender, class, ability (physical and mental), ethnicity, or native language to interrogate how systems function (i.e., whether they are advantaging or disadvantaging) based on experiential, observational, and empirical data.

Racial Equity: A lens of analysis that centers race to interrogate how systems function based on experiential, observational, and empirical data. Racial equity is the condition that would be achieved if one's race identity no longer predicted how one thrives in school and in life.

Social Justice: The idea that everyone deserves a right to succeed by having access to economic, political, and social rights and opportunities.

Structural Inequality: Characterized by the confluence of systems (education, criminal, legislative, health, etc.) created with roles, functions, decisions, rights, and opportunities designed for those who have typically sat in positions of power and have typically been identified as White with no regard that the adverse outcomes continuously disservice individuals of color, in particular, Black and Brown individuals.

Systemic Racism: While systemic racism and institutional racism are often terms used interchangeably, we proffer the ideas are distinctly different. Systemic racism can be defined as the infrastructure of government with laws, statutes, ordinances, and so on, that promulgate the rights and privileges of the people. The fabric of our society was established through a system of laws, statutes, and ordinances that declared some were better than others, that some had more rights than others. Today, the laws may no longer exist but the longstanding beliefs that undergirded these laws are alive—they linger and are evident in every facet of American life.

Systems of Oppression: Phrase used to identify inequity by naming the historical, organized, and intentional patterns of mistreatment of certain populations. In this book, the specific population we call attention to is Black and Brown individuals; however, there is a long and dark history of marginalization of many other intersectional populations in these United States of America.

White Supremacy Culture/White Dominant Culture (Eurocentric Culture): A historically based, institutionally perpetuated system of exploitation and oppression of people of color by

White people/European nations for the purpose of upholding normative ways of being and doing to maintain and defend a system of wealth, power, and privilege.

How the Book Is Organized

The organization of this book has been thoughtfully designed. The authors include three sections for readers that correspond to three spaces we expect readers to experience when interacting with this text: (1) the reflecting space (Chapters 1–3), (2) the making meaning space (Chapters 4–5), and (3) the doing space (Chapters 6–9).

While the authors present the chapters in a sequential order, the ideas are emergent and presented in a way to support the intersectional racial equity framework introduced in Chapter 2. Further, it is important that we, as authors, explicitly name that this book advances an intersectional racial equity framework and not a diversity, equity, and inclusion framework. We believe that our collective humanity requires more than what traditional diversity, equity, and inclusion efforts suggest (more than diverse hires, more than purchasing diverse textbooks, more than approving contracts with vendors of color, etc.). Of course, we think increased diversity and inclusion efforts are components of the overall work; however, these components must be carefully and thoughtfully integrated into a larger, more complex end goal. As six unapologetic Black women, we, the authors, bring our whole selves to this work. In our writing, our experiences and perspectives come from living and breathing in Black skin and dwelling on this earth as cisgender women. Hence, we joyously uplift the voices of Black, Brown, and Native/Indigenous lives, experiences, and struggles in this work. We can unequivocally pronounce that **it is not enough** to simply engage in "check it off" diversity and inclusion effort (refer to the brief list of diversity and inclusion efforts described earlier, if needed).

Finally, the authors deliberately integrated academic and conversational language throughout this book. This integration may occur within a chapter, and/or some chapters may lean toward one disposition or the other. The ultimate goal is to invoke access. For some readers, the academic language is more accessible, whereas conversational language, for others, is best. The authors acknowledge and broadly name that language convention is about access and not intellect. Our hope is to create a pathway to understand, disrupt, and then transform practice with the goal of healing—healing so we might cohere a collective humanity. The authors not only have a moral imperative, we have a survival imperative. We simply cannot continue in a world that dehumanizes others—it is unhealthy, unethical, and unlivable. The events of 2020 and 2021, to date, illustrate this point more than any words on a page can!

Part I

Beginning the Journey - The Reflecting Space

Race Matters Because Racism Does

1

The Tale of Two Kindergartners

Just imagine the excitement of the first day of "real school." Both Michael and Jonathan are 5-year-old, inquisitive young scholars. They are elated that today marks their first day of school with the "big kids." Both are up early to start their first day of kindergarten. You can feel the synergy in the homes of both boys, and you can sense their pure joy to meet all of their fellow classmates for the first day of official learning. While there are many similarities associated with this day for these two boys, there are distinct differences as well.

Meet Michael

Michael is a smart, active, and delightful 5-year-old prince. He is so thrilled to leave Grandma Lucy's house to finally attend school. While Grandma Lucy always had scheduled activities such as walks to the park and cartoon time, Michael was happy to begin learning to read and write his name like his big sisters. Therefore, when it finally came time for the first day of kindergarten, Michael was beaming. At 7:00 am on the first day of school, Michael's big sister Elizabeth had him up, dressed, and fed with one frosted strawberry Pop-Tart, his favorite. Cheryl, his mother, arrived home at 7:15 am. She was rushing in from the graveyard shift. There was no way Cheryl would miss taking Michael to his school for his first day of kindergarten. However, she was drained upon arriving home from work. She worked a double the day before, as raising three children as a single mother presents financial challenges. Accordingly, all additional funds were needed.

As Cheryl walked Michael to school, they discussed his hopes for the first day. Since times were tight, Cheryl could not obtain his school supplies for the first day, but they discussed all the items she should purchase on Friday, payday. When they arrived at the school, Cheryl stopped by the office to pick up a free backpack with generic school supplies. The school previously communicated this process for parents/guardians, like Cheryl, who were unable to secure a book bag and supplies before the first day of school. When Michael entered the classroom, he was beaming. He met Ms. Tallador. She was a young and kind teacher. She took Michael's book bag and gave him a gigantic hug. Then Ms. Tallador began talking to Cheryl. Simultaneously, she asked Michael to look for his name on the desk. Four minutes later, Ms. Tallador noticed Michael in the back of the room, crying. She went over to ask why he was crying, and he said he could not find his name because he did not know exactly how to spell his name yet. Michael said Grandma Lucy told him he would learn how to read and write when he got to real school. Ms. Tallador bent down and gave Michael a heartfelt hug. Then, she whispered into Michael's ear, saying, "You will learn how to write your name and so much more this school year."

Meet Jonathan

Jonathan is an active, inquisitive, and kind 5-year-old future artist. The first day of kindergarten was finally here. Since 2 years of age, Jonathan had been waiting for this day. Although he had been in a Montessori Early Learning Center for three years, he knew that kindergarten was the real deal. It was formal school, and it was the time when he could begin attending school with his older brother, Martin. At 5:00 am Mary was up early preparing lunches for Jonathan, Martin, and Timothy, her husband. Soon after lunches were made, Mary started preparing breakfast. She was determined to prepare Jonathan's favorite blueberry pancakes, sausage, and a tall glass of apple juice. At 6:30 am, Mary began singing, "It is the first day of school, it is the first day of school," as she walked into Jonathan's room to wake him up. Jonathan popped up and yelled, "Mommy, it is finally here!" As the family ate breakfast at the dining room table, Timothy kissed the children and Mary and excused himself early. He had an early meeting at work but apologized for missing taking Jonathan to the first day of kindergarten. However, he promised to pick him up after school. As Timothy left, Mary promised to take tons of pictures throughout the day as she already signed up to be a room parent. Therefore, she would be present for the entire day, helping the teacher, supervising the café during all three lunch shifts, and supporting the librarian in the afternoon. Mary and the boys left the house around 8:15 am. The boys' elementary school was not in the neighborhood; their special admit elementary school was a 30-minute drive from their house.

Upon arrival at school, Jonathan and Martin scurried to their class-rooms, as the school held several pre-first day events such as an ice cream social, a mix and mingle, and a school carnival. For each event, students were able to meet their teacher and classmates, visit their classrooms, and tour the school. Therefore, Jonathan already knew exactly where to go. Notwithstanding Jonathan's comfort level, he was stopped by three adults to make sure he did not need assis-tance. Upon arrival at the classroom, Jonathan placed his items in his locker. He immediately grabbed his just-right reading book from the class library and joined his friends on the rug near the "read and chill" center. Jonathan's teacher, Ms. Battlefield, had already screened students, and Jonathan was pre-determined to be in the highest reading group. His group actually went into one of the first-grade classrooms for reading class.

We are almost one quarter into the 21st century, yet so many of our youngest learners have starkly different experiences. Here, we have two children, Michael and Jonathan, who live in the same city, are the same age, and are in the same grade, yet they arrive at kin-dergarten with two uniquely different sets of lived experiences and school expectations. Michael, a White American student, lives on the west side of town. His mother, Cheryl, is a single parent. She is determined to raise her three children well on her annual sal-ary of $24,000. Graduating top of her high school class, Cheryl lives with her mother, Lucy, who serves as the core of her support system. Jonathan, a Black American, lives downtown with both of his parents and his brother. Mary, Jonathan's mother, is a stay-at-home mother. Mary and Timothy decided that Mary would quit her job as an accountant to stay at home with the children. Notwith-standing this family decision, their annual household income is still over $125,000.

In "The Tale of Two Kindergartners," there is a layered texture associated with each student. This texture accounts for the wide variance in experiences shared among and between many of America's public school students. For example, Michael did not have any formal early learning experience, whereas Jonathan attended a Montessori Early

Learning Center. Although there are some personal non-financial reasons many elect not to expose their children to a formal learning experience, many simply cannot afford this often costly expense. Here, Michael was not afforded any previous introductions to his new elementary school, yet Jonathan was exposed to several summer engagement activities. Understanding context and routines are two vital components for students to connect to and relate to learning experiences. Additionally, Michael's parent worked long hours, requiring him to spend a significant amount of time with his loving grandmother and helpful older sister. On the other hand, Jonathan had two parents, and one parent was a college-educated stay-at-home parent. Although Michael was White and Jonathan was Black, you might be tempted, at first glance, to describe Michael and Jonathan's experiences based on their socio-economic/class status. Before jumping to that conclusion, consider a new study from Stanford, Harvard, and U.S. Census Bureau economists that states that inequalities, primarily between Black Americans and White Americans, cannot be explained by socio-economic status/class (Chetty et al., 2018). Although discussing outcomes in terms of socio-economic status/class is more comfortable for many, we must challenge ourselves to be uncomfortable and truly contend with what report after report and statistic after statistic reveal. Race, unfortunately, is a keen predictor of a student's likelihood to read by third grade, graduate from high school, and avoid adverse interactions with the criminal justice system (Aud et al., 2010; Carson, 2015; Neill et al., 2014). What we know is this:

- Despite Jonathan having a parent available all day to support him,

- Despite Jonathan's parents being financially stable,

- Despite Jonathan's parents being college-educated, and

- Despite Jonathan having the benefit of two in-home parents available to support and love him,

Jonathan is three times less likely than Michael to be reading proficiently in the fourth grade (Annie E. Casey Foundation, 2014). Jonathan will not be treated by society in the same way as Michael. Jonathan will not have the same opportunities, and he will not be afforded access to high-quality education in schools that see his Blackness as an asset instead of a deficit.

When you sit with this information for a moment, you might, like us, become deeply troubled. The sad and the indisputable reality is race matters only because racism does. The issue of Jonathan and Michael's respective races would be inconsequential if they weren't about to enter a system that was intentionally designed to favor White individuals (irrespective of socio-economic status) over their Black counterparts. Even knowing "The Tale of Two Kindergartners," some Americans will still ponder these questions: Why must we dwell upon racism if we are finally living in a post-racial society? Haven't we progressed beyond that as a nation? The two-term presidency of Barack Obama, the first African American president of these United States of America, is often advanced as proof of our post-racial society. While President Obama's tenure inspired many, it concurrently revealed an unprecedented increase in public and unambiguous anti-Black messages.

Through a close examination of America's history, evidence of the horrendous treatment of individuals based on race, gender, gender orientation, sexual orientation, sexual identity, immigration status, religion, and/or disability is well documented (Painter, 2010). However, the treatment of individuals based on race—through the institution of racism—has forever tarnished the legacy of America's founding fathers, coupled with the legacies of many subsequent local, state, and national leaders. Accordingly, to explain why race matters because racism does, we will use the experience of White and Black people in America to solidify our message. Using a historical account, we maintain that understanding the White/Black binary in exploring racism in America is essential to our efforts to cohere our collective humanity.

We Must Begin at the Beginning

Guyatt (2016) and Painter (2010) provide a provocative historical account of the treatment of Indigenous individuals, African enslaved individuals, and select voluntary and involuntary immigrants. This treatment was initiated, allowed and maintained through the system of racism. To that end, a review of American history documents how the socially constructed idea of racism permeates the thinking, being, and living of most (if not all) Americans (Wilkerson, 2020). We should pause and norm the idea that race, for us, is a social construction and not a biological reality. Our thinking is aligned to Wilkerson (2020). There are no genes associated with race. Instead, race is a human classification system used to justify racism.

From the first documented Spanish settlement in the 1400s to the first documented English settlement in 1600s and then to this precise moment in history, how non-White settlers were treated served as a blueprint of how to advance racially involved and/or motivated political, economic, and social actions (Taylor & Foner, 2002).

Consider the following: The Declaration of Independence states, in relevant part,

> We hold these truths to be self-evident, that all men are created equal, that they are endowed by their Creator with certain unalienable Rights that among these are Life, Liberty, and the pursuit of Happiness. That to secure these rights, Governments are instituted among Men, deriving their just powers from the consent of the governed. (Jefferson, 1774)

Pause and Reflect

Consider how a nation could be created without regard for those who were present and occupied the land first.

Consider how a nation could be created without regard for those who helped to build this nation, the enslaved Africans.

Consider what messages had to be communicated to justify such actions.

Although the preceding excerpt reads "all men," the reality is, at the time of the signing of the Declaration of Independence, Africans were enslaved. This race-based enslavement was supported by the ideology that the Black/African enslaved individuals were "less than" their White counterparts. This 1774 ideology perpetuated the system of institutional racism, a system that has endured over the course of centuries of American history and continues to this day. Further, 16 years later, the Nationalization Act of 1790, outlined criteria for granting citizenship in the United States of America (Hannah-Jones et al., 2019). The provisions for citizenship excluded

Indigenous individuals, enslaved individuals, free Black people/ Africans, indentured servants, and all Asians. Only individuals who were "free White . . . and of good character" were eligible for citizenship (Coulson, 2015).

The Thirteenth Amendment, enacted in 1865, abolished slavery except as "as punishment for a crime" (Alexander, 2010). This was a *technical solution* (Heifetz et al., 2009) to address institutional racism, which at the time, exclusively impacted enslaved Africans. Our nation's history reveals all too many instances in which such technical solutions didn't pinpoint the root causes of the challenge. Typically, the flaws of technical solutions fall into two categories that often co-exist: (1) Those who benefit by sustaining the status quo often find "workarounds" that subvert the intent of the technical fix, and (2) such solutions are superficial in that they simply do not disrupt the systems (in this case, institutional racism) that are at heart of the problem.

The first such "workaround" can be traced back to the period following the passage of the Thirteenth Amendment, a constitutional amendment that was designed to abolish slavery. Almost immediately after the federal legislation went into effect, multiple states instituted the Black Codes, the first manifestation of Jim Crow laws and a mechanism to restrict the freedoms of Black people/Africans (Alexander, 2010) and to compel them to work for low wages. Not only was race used legislatively, but it was also pronounced boldly through the judicial system, including the highest court in the land. Contemplate the rulings of the Supreme Court, of these United States of America, for example. In the landmark cases of *Dred Scott v. John F.A. Sandford*, 60 U.S. 393 (1857) and *Plessy v. Ferguson*, 163 U.S. 537 (1896), the judicial system was used to extend the race-based laws that legally solidified the hierarchy of individuals based on the socially constructed idea known as race. In the former case, the highest court ruled in a 7–2 decision that the U.S. Constitution was not intended to protect Black individuals (enslaved or free). In the latter case, the highest court ruled in a 7–1 decision that Black individuals were not entitled to interact in public spaces with White individuals and ultimately declared that separate but equal public accommodations were legal (Klarman, 2004). Although the *Brown v. Board of Education of Topeka*, 347 U.S. 483 (1954) eventually overturned the 1896 "separate but equal" doctrine, keep in mind that it took 68 years to overturn the *Plessy* decision and 114 years to overturn the *Scott* decision, and the decision was still a technical solution in that the implementation of school desegregation didn't change the root cause of the problem, which was institutional racism.

Today, the mass incarceration of Black and Brown individuals closely resembles the impact of the Black Codes. This striking similarity is analyzed critically in Michelle Alexander's *The New Jim Crow* (Alexander, 2010). Once again, the technical solution of the Thirteenth Amendment was subverted by workarounds like the Black Codes/Jim Crow laws, higher rates of criminal prosecution for Black and Brown individuals, and mandatory sentencing requirements for crimes frequently associated with Black and Brown communities that have endured to the present day.

Although we've only presented a glimpse into the manner in which race and White supremacy have been woven into the fabric of our country's history, by now it should be clear that the social construction of race, as well as its subsequent use to solidify institutional racism, systems of oppression, and systems of privilege, have had a profound impact on all facets of American life. The most prominent display of why race matters can be realized by examining our nation's carefully constructed and intentionally designed public education and mass communication/media systems.

How Race Influenced the Development of Our Public School System

Monica, a Black female, sat down to have her exit interview with the 12th-grade counselor, Mrs. Green, who is Black. Mrs. Green told Monica that although she had successfully completed all of her high school requirements with honors, it was best that she look for a steady job or consider the military rather than college because after all "none of the kids from this neighborhood go to college because they mostly end up just working somewhere."

This brief, but all too common story—Black children being limited by the dominant narrative informing who they can or cannot be—is yet another powerful reminder of why race matters. Race matters because systemic racism continues to uphold laws, policies, and societal norms that pre-determine the value and visibility of Black people Whether you are White or even Black, like Monica's 12th-grade counselor, the socialization of Whiteness reaches all. If you are not conscious of this socialization, you will unconsciously, or even consciously, inflict the marginalization of others. To understand the gravity of the impact of the history of America and its direct influence on public education, we must first admit that the Black experience was poisoned by the direct and indirect results of slavery. Race matters when examining the public education system because once Black people were able to legally gain access to a free education, they were unwelcomed and purposefully disadvantaged. These disadvantages were not due to happenstance but were a by-product of a system of laws that directly hindered fair and equal access to a free education for Black people, thus upholding and sustaining systemic racism. In 1933, Carter G. Woodson stated that "to handicap a student as by teaching him that his Black face is a curse and that his struggle to change his condition is hopeless is the worst sort of lynching" (p. 8). When you combine the blatant disregard for the lives of Black people that has endured for hundreds of years with an educational system that consistently failed to create a safe psychological or physical space, the result is academic learning gaps and an overall sense of exclusion. The simple idea of changing the reality of the Black experience in public education requires nothing less than an abrupt and direct confrontation with and dismantling of systemic racism.

In the midst of our current "post-truth" era, we urge you to critically examine the historical and contemporary realities of the Black experience in public education. The facts are abundantly clear. After the 1954 ruling in *Brown v. Board of Education of Topeka*, American schools were legally mandated to integrate. Consequentially, the court ruling was met with a massive amount of opposition. Over 20 years later, after some states blatantly attempted to ignore the court's ruling, buses of Black people students had to be escorted to school by police escorts.

This type of psychological and physical warfare has only one goal, and that is to destroy the basic premise of education for the Black student. Black people were legally owed a free (meaning of no cost), public (provided by the government versus a private institution) education. For clarity, the previous statement means that all American children, regardless of race and/or socio-economic status, should be able to "leave school with skills that position them to compete fairly and productively in the nation's democratic governance and occupational structure" (Rothstein, 2004, p. 1).

Pause and Reflect

Reflect on your educational experience, and racialize your experience as a student. What were your racial noticings?

Reflect on the curriculum that you were exposed to during your educational experience: Were the experiences of people of color acknowledged? If so, were their stories made visible from an inclusive standpoint, or did you have to infer?

Reflect on the overall subliminal messages you received during your educational experience. Did you feel like the education system was designed to promote your overall academic and psychological success? If not, why?

The educational journey of Black people in the context of systemic racism in this country is much like a qualified runner participating in a race for their psychological, emotional, academic, and physical freedom. Regardless of (or perhaps because of) their qualifications, they are forced to start 300 meters behind their White opponents. The 300-meter deficit could be defined through the lens of racism as continuous exposure to segregated schools, problematic curriculums that purposefully promote "race invisibility," high teacher turnover that results in a lack of rigorous and innovative instruction, and the absence of high expectations for success. To confront and disrupt the systemic racism that upholds the ills of public education, we must examine its inception, continuous equity disparities, and how it is marketed in the media.

Race and Racism Shape the Media's Message

A California teacher was placed on leave for a second time after allegedly telling students she wanted to "bring back slavery" and making other racist remarks. (DailyMail.com, 2019)

Black Alabama students and parents are speaking out after a student leaked a teacher group chat, calling one student the n-word and denigrating another's intelligence. (Defender News Service, 2019)

A New York school district is being hit with a lawsuit over a racist slideshow allegedly created by a science teacher. WCBS-TV reports the slideshow featured a photo of four Black students on a class trip to the Bronx Zoo, and one of a gorilla, and the label "Monkey see, monkey do." (CBS News, 2020)

These headlines are not fake news. Racism is consistently communicated through various media platforms. These stories are among the many shared through national media outlets. But, to further elaborate on the theme of this chapter, race matters in the media because racism matters and negatively impacts Black people daily. One might argue that these news stories expose the presence of racism in our schools, yet we must also remember that a Black person's character, ability, and/or behavior is pre-determined based on socially fabricated indicators of difference rooted in White supremacy. The impact of racism through personal, structural, or systemic actions founded on a premise of predictions based on a person's race is evidenced in our daily consumption of information from the media. If you are a Black or Brown student in an American school, you are likely to experience the impact of national media stories. Like the educators who were hired to serve them, Black and Brown students are not shielded from the influence of the media's messages.

Pause and Reflect

Consider the last five news updates you watched.

- How was race used and/or disregarded in the framing of each of these stories?

- What words were used to describe the individuals in the stories?

- What conclusions were drawn?

As advocates of children, we appreciate the media bringing to awareness the injustices suffered by students. However, it is the same media that consistently provide messages steeped in racism, which does harm to the same students. There are some scholars, such as William Julius Wilson and Roland Fryer, who would argue that if you are a Black person, today your life has less racism and discrimination. The national media stories captured earlier in this section do not support that Black students are experiencing a world with less racism and bigotry. The media's daily portrayal of Blackness perpetuates and profits from the disenfranchisement of Black people. The media's influence on the narrative of race and racism cannot be ignored, specifically its influence on teachers and how that subsequently impacts Black and Brown students.

The media's impact on ideas and values is not a new phenomenon. Historically, the media have influenced shared ideologies, biases, and how we negotiate our values. This historical influence has always been steeped in a narrative created by the dominant White culture. From its inception, the media's messages have been ingrained with racial prejudices, racial bias, and racial discrimination resulting in a legacy of racism. "Communities of color have been targeted and harmed by fake news and media manipulation since colonial times" (Torres, 2018). The White dominant culture controlled media and subsequently commanded the images portrayed of all Black people. With no ability to control the narrative, Black people struggled to represent their beliefs, identities, and stories accurately. For example, there was a propaganda poster from World War I that advertised the U.S. Army using an image of a menacing Black gorilla gripping a bloody club with one hand. In an attack stance, the Black gorilla stands with bloody hands while cupped in its arms appears to be a barely covered White woman in distress. The title of the poster, created by Harry R. Hopps in 1917, was "Destroy This Mad Brute." Fast-forward to 2008, when *Vogue* magazine's first Black male graces the cover. If you look at the "Destroy This Mad Brute" poster and the cover of the *Vogue* magazine, side by side, the image brings into question the message *Vogue* was attempting to communicate regarding the first time a Black man graced the cover of the popular magazine (https://www.thefashionspot.com/runway-news/439187-controversial-vogue-covers-published/3/). LeBron James seems to emulate the Black gorilla, who is seen as a brute or savage from the "Destroy This Mad Brute" predecessor. On the *Vogue* cover, the bloody club is replaced with a basketball, and the distressed White woman is substituted with super model Gisele Bündchen. Gisele's teal-colored dress is the same colored dress as the distressed White woman from "Destroy This Mad Brute." The visual perpetuates the negative imaging of Black athletes. It is also a reminder that it took 116 years for the first Black man to be on the cover of *Vogue* in 2008. In a mainstream, world-renowned magazine, Black male beauty was not worthy of the front cover, and when it was acknowledged, it was compared to a Black gorilla, an animal. In this example of print media, the media's message is blatant, and instead of the platform being used to dismantle systems of oppression, the racist depiction attempts to legitimize the hostility and fear toward Black men.

As educators, we have a thirst for information, and the media provide an endless faucet of flowing information. What is the impact on students of color and teachers when they are bombarded with stories that demonstrate the marginalization and oppression experienced by Black and Brown people?

Malcolm X (n.d.) described the media's influence as "the most powerful entity on earth. They have the power to make the innocent guilty and to make the guilty innocent, and that's power. Because they control the minds of the masses." As we transcend 61 years to 2021, Malcolm X's quote seems timeless, especially if you are Black.

Ideas to Sit With

Being shot for having your hood up and walking home with Skittles

Having your death ruled a suicide when you are shot while handcuffed in the back of a police patrol car

Being 14 years old and choked to the point of urinating on yourself because of a look you gave police

During a pandemic, being profiled by police for being in a store with a mask covering your mouth and nose

Being perceived as King Kong, a brute, a savage

Being killed while sleeping in your bed

As an educator, the influence of the media's messages on you do not magically disappear when the school day begins. Just as the media can be used to generate profit, it can also be used to marginalize through a repeated constructed narrative. For Black students, the media's influence of repeated racially constructed narratives can have an impact on their academic reality. In a research study conducted by Dixon (2017), representations of families by race were examined through television, print, and online. The findings revealed these constructed, distorted narratives for Black families (Dixon, 2017):

- More Black families live in poverty than White families.

- Black people utilize public government assistance because of laziness, drug dependency, or dysfunction.

- Black fathers are not present in the lives of their children.

- Black single mothers make bad decisions related to relationships.

- Black families are associated with crime.

- Black families are not stable.

Information communicated through the media can impact how people construct social identities and realities for others outside of their race group. When people have little knowledge, background, or experience related to race, the messages delivered by the media become their framework for making meaning of the world. This framework is especially dangerous when the information being shared enhances the systemic subjugation of Black and Brown people. These audiences rely on the media to shape their reality and in the absence of a counternarrative, the distortions of White dominant messaging become that reality (Happer & Philo, 2013). How might a distorted narrative of Black families impact the treatment of Black students?

Research supports the correlation between repeated negative stereotypes and Black people in the media. These negative stereotypes often highlight deficit attitudes and beliefs about intelligence, values, family structures, criminality, socio-economic status, and the ability of Black people to achieve (e.g., Dixon, 2007; Mastro & Kopacz, 2006; Tan et al., 2000). In 2011, research conducted by the Opportunity Agenda provided specific data associated with the impact of negative mass media on Black males. The study indicated a "troubling link between media portrayals and lowered life chances for Black males" (p. 13). Donaldson (2015) further analyzed the data and added clarity to our understanding of the media's impact on the lives of Black males.

Given this dynamic, students of color internalize these negative messages from media about the diminished potential of Black boys, and this contributes to *actual* diminished potential—a self-fulfilling prophecy. Consequently, Black boys who may in fact have great potential internalize the negative messaging to the point they follow the "script." The effect, if not addressed, manifests not only in lower academic achievement but future implications of denied jobs, declined loans, and a continued pervasive antagonism toward Black boys, who eventually become Black men. All the more reason that we must cultivate an understanding of the power dynamic in our collective effort to dismantle systems and structures that were never designed for the benefit of Black and Brown students.

Racism is real. It is a daily exhausting experience for people of color. This chapter sets the stage for how racism through institutionalized policies and practices is deeply rooted in our history, in our education systems, and through how we communicate. The complexities of racism and its impact on the outcomes for people of color require an approach just as textured to address those complexities. In subsequent chapters, you will develop an understanding of the conscious anti-racist engendering (CARE) framework. The CARE framework is a thoughtful systemic approach to uproot and advance the capacity to engage in the work of dismantling racism with the goal of collectively disrupting systems of oppression.

What Nobody Talks About

The stories told to us by our community, public and private institutions, the media, and history reinforce the complex system of racism. These stories were created by design and must be deconstructed with the same sense of intentionality.

Your Lived Experience

Your lived experiences inform your worldview.

- How have your lived experiences impacted your perspective of racism in America?

- Do you readily see and/or experience issues of racism in your daily lived experience? If your answer is yes, how do you respond to these observations/experiences? If you answer is no, why do you believe this is the case?

Chapter Reflection

- How does "The Tale of Two Kindergartners" speak to what you know about inequalities in our nation's school communities?

- In terms of student outcomes, are you challenged by the idea that when race and class intersect, race typically serves as the driving factor? Reflect on your thinking.

- In the past, have you experienced any events that required you to reflect upon racial dynamics of all those involved in a particular situation?

- What happened that promoted you to notice the racial dynamics?

- When was the last time you noticed a racial inequity in your classroom, school, and/or workplace? How did your address the racial inequity?

- Do you recall a time when you tapped into racial bias to inform your decision making? What can you do differently to be more self-aware in the future?

- What systemic racist practices have you observed during your time as a student or educator?

- Considering the idea that the public school system was not designed for the academic or psychological advancement of Black students, how can you use your positional power to disrupt on their behalf?

Building Community by Reimagining New Possibilities 2

Jessica was a recent graduate of Howard University School of Journalism. She longed for the opportunity to work for an organization that specialized in highlighting issues about race and gender inequality. So, it was safe to say she was beyond elated when she was offered an entry-level position as a junior reporter for an urban publication that sought to share empowering stories of women from all different walks of life. It only took a few weeks of field training and staff meetings for Jessica to notice an observable pattern about the narratives that were told about women of color versus those who were White. As she built relationships with various colleagues, the watercooler talk verified that she wasn't alone in her observations, but no one ever shared their feelings during the weekly staff meetings, which were led by the all-White executive leadership team. These meetings began to feel suffocating to Jessica because she felt like her heart's desire and lived experience as a Black woman was being ignored and erased by the organization's historical storytelling practices, which were steeped in uplifting stereotypical stories about Black women, with no investment in engaging in authentic multiple perspectives. During one staff meeting Jessica conjured up the courage to ask the question, "Why are we always telling the same stories about the same type of women?" Margie, the lead executive team member, quickly responded by saying, "Jess, we tell the stories we know the people know and expect to hear." Two weeks later Jessica handed in her letter of resignation.

Jessica's story is not an anomaly, and often organizations that were created with the best of intentions hardly ever engage in practices that would eliminate systems that silence the voices of those within its community. Dr. Martin Luther King Jr. (1966) stated, "Our goal is to create a beloved community that will require a qualitative change in our souls as well as a quantitative change in our lives." Creating the "beloved community" is essential work when striving to eradicate systematic racism. Racism will never be interrupted as long as our organizations cling to systems and structures that were designed to serve the dominant culture. Traditional models of leadership often call upon us to invest an inordinate amount of time developing and implementing strategic plans. There are different names for these documents; for example, in the field of education we would refer to the School Improvement Plans, or in the not- or for-profit world it would be the Organizational Effectiveness Plan. Irrespective of what they are called, the sole purpose of these documents is to move the work of the organization based on its vision, desired data metrics, and anticipated outcomes. Often the vision of the organization (as outlined in these plans) is conceived in a vacuum by those who are a part of the dominant culture and have positional power. Further, the data metrics are often narrow in focus and based on isolated data points such as standardized scores rather than the rich, descriptive data that can be collected through qualitative methods. Plans organized in this way are problematic and highly positioned to replicate White supremacy culture. Imagine a car manufacturer creating the same car year after year with the same manufacturing defect and wondering why customer loyalty is tanking. Planning and organizing in absence of examination is bound to produce the same outcomes and issues that will cost deeply over time. Moreover, when the planners are limited to those with positional power (usually those in the dominant majority), the process typically suffers from an emphasis on a sense of urgency and quantity over quality. In addition to urgency and quantity over quality, White supremacist thinking normalizes specific ways of making meaning of our world, including the following:

1. Valuing product over process ("The ends justify the means.")

2. Overemphasis on perfectionism ("There is no room for errors." "There is only one right way.")

3. Binary (either/or) thinking ("It's either black or white." "You're either with us or against us.")

Since the Eurocentric cultural lens leaves little room for the nuance or the complexities of race, we want to propose a counternarrative. Let us reimagine an organization seeking to develop and implement a strategic plan that is entrenched in anti-racist practices. What might that look like? What type of practices would be important to observe? Consider Jessica's experience. What might an anti-racist organization's response to her wonders sound like? What type of practices would have been put in place prior to her arrival that would be easy to observe? This chapter will describe the *conscious anti-racist engendering (CARE) framework* as a tool for engaging planning for anti-racist operations, specifically highlighting the first steps of the model, community building and normalizing adult learning.

Figure 2.1   Conscious Anti-Racist Engendering (CARE) Framework

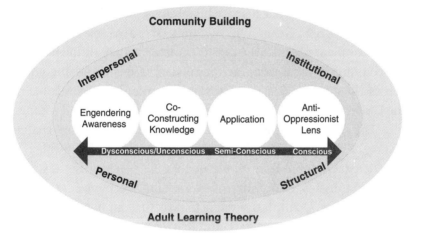

Dismantling oppressive organizational practices requires both skillful change management and focused capacity building. Further, these efforts, organizational transformation, and capacity building should have a framework of accountability. The CARE framework provides a way to consider these goals as it undertakes the work of intersectional anti-racism. This will require the organization to not just consider race but also how it intersects with other facets of a person's identity such as gender, class, or native language. Identifying this as intersection does two things: First, it names what is real and obvious for the sake of discussion and not persecution, and second, it gives credence to the biases and stereotypes so that a true disruption of racial practices can be examined. The framework is designed to constellate around two essential questions: (1) How do we build community? (2) How do we normalize adult learning as a mode of operations in the organization? Consider these two questions in the context of traditional strategic planning exercises and how the CARE framework makes the process different than traditional approaches.

First, in traditional models, the community members with the most influence are usually those with power and authority. This power can be derived by position and/or connections with organizational capital. All voices are not treated equally, and all perspectives are not valued. Typically, the equation skews toward those with power having the most influence during the planning processes. In contrast, leaders who apply the CARE framework purposefully center and grant authority to those who are marginalized, those whom the organization is there to serve, those whose experiences are often excluded. The positional power of the leader is deployed in service of creating conditions that disrupt hierarchies that perpetuate structural forms of oppression. While we underscore the role of the leader with positional power, we want to emphasize that all members of the community must examine the concept of democratizing power across the community. The vision of community undergirded by the CARE framework might best be described as a beloved community. The community model employed by CARE framework centers justice-based interpersonal and community-based relationships. In the context of CARE framework, qualitative encompasses a way of being that invites a full range of expression, acceptance, and value of all identities. Quantitative refers to divesting our oppressive practices and holding ourselves accountable for making repairs and reparations when needed.

An anti-racist organization must be willing to commit to creating transparent and recursive protocols that advance anti-racist practices. Before this can happen, we must acknowledge that the beliefs, traditions, and actions that form our status quo are steeped in racist practices; rather than applying the technical fixes or workarounds discussed in the prior chapter, we must *reimagine* our organization. For example, the organization's vision must explicitly state a true commitment to pursuing anti-racism. Its stakeholders must represent a range of racial groups that are directly impacted by the work of the organization both internally and externally. The data metrics should be equally if not be more geared toward placing an emphasis on qualitative data collection over quantitative data collection. Community building can greatly benefit our efforts to create anti-racist leadership and organizations.

Normalizing Adult Learning as a Means of Achieving Anti-Racist Functioning

Dismantling institutional racism necessitates sustained professional learning. Leaders and teams must commit to interrogating the manner in which they internalize oppressive ways of being and knowing. Such deep-seated change will not be leveraged with "spray and pray" workshops. It can take several years of concerted effort on the part of all members of the community to chip away at White supremacist beliefs and paradigms. Adults with advanced degrees, decades of experience, and stellar reputations in the field must be as willing to be a part of this process as well as fledgling professionals. This is what the outer concentric circle of the CARE framework is meant to depict.

Pause and Reflect

Consider the organization you work for, and now reimagine it using an anti-racist lens. Reflect on what organizational practices will need to be disrupted immediately. What role can you play in this disruption?

Building Community by Examining Our Individual Racial Identities

The term *community* speaks to a collection of people joined together by some common interest. In the words of Dr. King, beloved communities are intentional about creating conditions in which multiple perspectives are honored and in which practices that are steeped in White supremacy culture may be challenged (Gray, 2019). Leaders must sit with how they perceive, engage with, define, and understand their racial identities. Ultimately, they must be able to discover and accept how their lived racialized experiences have shaped both their self-perceptions and their perceptions of others in their personal and professional lives. White people as well as people of color are expected to engage in this type of racial identity work. Dr. Beverly Tatum wrote, racism is "a system of advantage based on race, where White people are advantaged, and people of color are disadvantaged." Because racism is embedded within four interlocking forms of oppression—internal, interpersonal, institutional, ideological— White people must unlearn the belief that White supremacy exists only in interpersonal, explicit action (Greenia, 2018). For example, White people cannot selectively choose to not benefit from direct and indirect privileges they receive due to their race. Racism is complex, layered, and engrained in every aspect of the human existence.

Racial identity work should not be done in isolation but rather in communion with the participants within the organization. It requires more than self-reflection in a silo, or random self-examination activities devoid of opportunities to gain multiple perspectives. Individuals must take an active role in examining their own cultures and the influence of those cultures on the construction of their racial identities. At the same time, we must strive to gain perspectives from others' lived experiences. Without this intentional self-examination, we will continue to be entrapped in thoughts, ideas, structures, and plans that reinforce the status quo and are harmful to the overall organization and its stakeholders. Reflecting on Jessica's experience, the lack of individual and collective examination yielded an experience that caused her to resign rather than stay and flourish. Lack of examination will continue to reproduce increased marginalization among those who sit in power versus those who labor.

The innovative nature of the CARE framework is the manner in which it depicts how community building creates space for all members of the community to examine trust and vulnerability, broker accountability for everyone's personal work, and understand the intended goal and outcomes of an anti-racist organization. There is a direct relationship between trust and vulnerability that, on its surface, can make any leader feel like they are entering a firing squad without a safety net or escape plan. At the same time, the rewards of this type of emancipation are invaluable. Dr. Brené Brown (2012) wrote, "Vulnerability is not weakness; it's our greatest measure of courage" and "trust is a product of vulnerability that grows over time and requires work, attention, and full engagement" (p. 53). This type of bold declaration starts with examining our individual responsibility, but it ultimately becomes the key to taking collective responsibility.

Mobilizing the Significance of Collective Responsibility

An anti-racist organization requires a commitment to transparency about our racial identities, willingness to be vulnerable with other members of the community, and trust in partners to work collaboratively to disrupt the workings of power and privilege. Collective work engenders brilliance and power. Every person enters the community with unique assets and interpersonal skills that help us communicate clearly and competently with others. We draw upon these personal and interpersonal skills to articulate our lived experience, particularly our understanding of how power and privilege impact our organizations. In such brave spaces, we can imagine and act upon ideas that disrupt and dismantle racist practices. Creating space for a meaningful dialogue is the gateway to liberating our organizations. It makes the difference between an organization that only makes statements about impending change and one that is committed to radical transformation. Organizational transformation will require revolutionary changes to policies and practices that were mostly beneficial to dominant culture. This cannot be done overnight nor without its members having the courage to identify their lack of understanding and awareness of how such policies and practices are racist.

Built on a foundation of adult learning research and theory, the CARE framework embodies a continuum of awareness and learning beginning with engendering awareness (dysconscious/unconscious – I don't know but I think I do, uncritical racialized knowing), to co-constructing knowledge, to application (semi-conscious – I know I don't know racially, and I am questioning), and ultimately developing an anti-oppressionist lens (consciousness – I know that I know racially). Note that the arrows in Figure 2.1 are bi-directional, suggesting that progress does not always occur in a one-way trajectory. An understanding of this growth process provides us with a common vocabulary to define and communicate how and what we are experiencing. We also rely on conversation protocols that allow for truth, transparency, and permission to create shared accountability.

Whether we enter the organization as the founder or a hired employee, we commit to engage in this work to promote anti-racism. While we may be inclined toward diplomacy and building a "culture of nice," we must recognize that such uninterrupted cultures are grounded in the many racist beliefs that hurt all people, especially those of color.

In fact, they rob White people of the opportunity to examine a false sense of privilege that has been bestowed upon them—a legacy of caste that began with the slave trade and institutionalized an unjust definition of property and power, and a well-entrenched false doctrine that was used to resist change. All of us have been impacted in some way by racism across generations. We have to interrupt it! Interruption starts within the community and, with diligent persistence, will change the institutional and structural systems that ultimately harm us all.

What Nobody Talks About

Anti-racism requires courage, perseverance, tenacity, and sacrifice. As you embark on the journey to be anti-racist, having a safe group of people who are outside of the organization will help serve as thought-partners who can aid in creating space to struggle, reflect, and grow.

Your Lived Experience

Your lived experiences shape who you are as a person and ultimately how you view and behave within your leadership role.

- Based on your title and those you influence, what commitment will you make to creating space for marginalized members of your organization's community to share their lived experiences?

Chapter Reflection

- What data metrics are your organization currently using to measure its effectiveness?

  o Are more quantitative metrics used versus qualitative metrics?

  o What is the racial makeup of the organization's community?

- How has your personal racial journey shaped how you engage within your organization?

  - Are you afforded space to share your racial identity journey and its implications on your role within the organization?

  - What marginalized groups sit within or are served by your organization?

    - How are they positioned within the organization?

    - Who are they? What type of voice do they have? How are data collected?

- Is there evidence of a change within the organization that shows transition to anti-racist practices?

Confronting Blame by Reframing Accountability 3

I have come to believe over and over again that what is most important to me must be spoken, made verbal and shared, even at the risk of having it bruised or misunderstood.

Audre Lorde

Our equity meetings make me feel . . . well . . . mostly uncomfortable, uncertain, and guilty. I am sure everyone notices how awkward these meetings are for me. In other settings with my same colleagues, I am engaging, and talking is not an issue. In the equity meetings, I feel conflicted, and I shut down. I often leave the meetings feeling shame for participating in systemic racist practices that hurt Black people. I struggle because I know I am more "woke" than most of my colleagues. I read books on race; I go to professional developments to better educate myself. I marched in a Black Lives Matter protest. I want this world to be a better place. Nevertheless, during the meetings, I sit in silence. I do not trust anyone enough to talk about my feelings or ask questions. I am conflicted because even when I know I should interrupt a racist discourse among colleagues, I do not. I smile, I nod, and I remain silent. I see how mean and disrespectful other colleagues are to Ms. Jackson, a Black faculty member on our team. Although I do not share in their mindset and behaviors, Ms. Jackson likely thinks I do . . . based on my silence in these meetings and their actions. With everything going on in this country, from riots to insurrections, I feel like I am walking on eggshells. My silence is a safer option than if I say something insensitive . . . if I do not recognize my privilege . . . or my worst nightmare, being called or thought of as a racist. My silence is my comfort, and I often choose this comfort to disengage from the group and the discussion.

The preceding sentiments indicate feelings shared by Ms. Tallador (Michael's teacher from "The Tale of Two Kindergartners") as she reflected on how her discomfort impacts her behavior, especially when race is the topic. Ms. Tallador's discomfort is amplified because, in the wake of a global pandemic, the country experienced a social pandemic. As the number of COVID-19 infections and deaths skyrocketed, with disproportionate caseloads among Black communities, Americans witnessed the murders of innocent Black people at the hands of the police. Rather than taking bold steps to address the root of such tragedies, political leaders opted for a different approach. In the fall of 2020, former president Donald Trump issued an executive order banning federal contractors from conducting racial sensitivity trainings. Using social media as a platform in conjunction with his power and influence, the former president shared with 88,776,124 followers that he viewed the participation and delivery of such trainings as "efforts to indoctrinate government employees with divisive and harmful sex and race-based ideologies" (Martin, 2020). These actions at the federal level showcased how power and influence maintain existing social order. Decisions at the macro level designed by those with the wealth, power, and privilege uphold normative ways of being created to continue the marginalization and oppression of people of color. Black students are not living in a bubble, free from the effects of federal policies, bias, prejudice, and racism. We need only pore over decades of disproportionate school and district data across multiple measures, including achievement, suspension rates, dropout rates, and over-referrals to special education services for students of color as evidence of how our school systems are complicit in their actions or lack thereof. School systems across the United States share an obligation to analyze and address years of racially discrepant data highlighting practices and policies steeped in racism. To state it more bluntly, our education system has consistently failed to educate all its students.

In Chapter 2, you learned the importance of creating the "beloved community" when eradicating structural racism. Ms. Tallador's reflection highlights the lack of community established to create space for all members. Failure to center social justice–based, interpersonal, and community-based relationships as the foundation for building community has resulted in systems that continue to struggle to reframe accountability in an environment heightened with racial and social unrest. Educators are entering into spaces, both physical and virtual, ill-equipped to improve outcomes for students of color.

It is not because they do not want to improve outcomes but because their capacity to engage in equity work has not been developed. It is not surprising that White educators often will lean into their comfort zones and avoid the discomfort of racialized situations, conversations, or meetings, especially if they perceive they will be challenged or identified as a racist. Building racial consciousness takes the will and skill to apply a racialized lens to our interactions with one another.

Equity work is not the job of one individual. The work is our shared responsibility, and each of us must be committed to disrupting the ideas and material manifestations of racism, such as racial disparities in education, health care, criminal justice, homeownership, and job opportunities, to name a few. It is more than opposing racist ideas and policies. Creating the conditions in which all stakeholders can address racial inequities is the charge. Enhancing this capacity adds to the power of the collective in transforming the cultures, policies, and practices that created and sustained adverse outcomes for generations of students of color (Galloway & Ishimaru, 2019). When creating conditions in which stakeholders build their capacity, we must understand the importance of trust and vulnerability as vital aspects of community building.

At the same time, we must also understand that building community is highly nuanced. It is not a race-neutral endeavor simply because racism exists because of race. Divorcing race from community building will inhibit authentic relationships. Once the conditions in which all stakeholders have the capacity to address racial inequities have been established, leaders can elevate and commit to an anti-racist culture in both work and learning environments.

Signs of a Culture of Blame

- A general lack of accountability on the team

- Hesitancy to admit mistakes or frequent attempts to hide mistakes versus fixing the mistake

- An overall lack of commitment to the excellence in the work or the needs of the students

- Persistent gossip and undermining of the goal or message

(Henry, 2020)

Being accountable and placing blame are not the same. When confronted with challenging issues, our natural tendency is to assign blame. Blaming somebody is more comfortable for most people than confronting the issue head on. When we have the courage to confront the issue, we begin to understand how racism lives in systems and practices and through people's intentional and unintentional actions. One of the most significant risks in advancing equity work is establishing a culture of blame, or a culture in which there is a toxic feeling between people of color and White people. Cultures of blame facilitate an environment where educators are unwilling to be accountable and committed to school-related goals, including equity-focused goals for students of color.

Blame is destructive to the community because it stagnates growth, learning, and the potential for change. Reframing accountability provides an opportunity to change the discourse associated with accountability from one rooted in shame and blame to one that works in the interest of better serving students and families. Reframing accountability offers the opportunity to change the discourse of accountability.

When leading for racial equity, you are working in the collective to advance educators on their equity journey to build consciousness and create the sense of urgency needed to improve outcomes for students of color. Each person is unique, and it is only through their willingness to express and examine their internal beliefs and biases that there can be any construction of collective agency. According to Hewson (2010), collective agency occurs when people are intentional, rational, and leverage their power to act or be responsive. Social movements, protests, and the dismantling of institutionalized racist practices are examples of collective agency. Collective agency must be built because the starting point for each individual's equity journey differs. Think of it as being with your team on a private jet. We are all traveling to the same destination (building our equity capacity). Still, everyone is boarding at different times, at different locations, with different racialized experiences that will influence our emerging equity capacity. Despite the differences, everyone is on the journey, and exiting the journey is not an option. With this in mind, there is purposeful foundational work needed requiring mindfulness of your consciousness and the consciousness of those within the community. This chapter will utilize the CARE framework to examine the importance of trust and vulnerability as functions of community building.

Pause and Reflect

Based on the list in "Signs of a Culture of Blame" (see page 37), evaluate if there is a culture of blame in your organization or among your team. How might a culture of blame impact your efforts to build community?

The Trust Exchange

Trust is the foundation upon which healthy relationships are built. In personal relationships, trust is established when we feel an assured reliance on others, and we are confident that they will speak the truth. Dr. Brené Brown, during a 2015 speech, articulated, "Trust is choosing to make something important to you vulnerable to the actions of someone else." This concept of trust also applies when building professional relationships that lead to and depend upon collaboration. Without trust, educators will not progress along their equity journeys. When leading for racial equity, we must strive to create trusted spaces free from negative judgment, where vulnerability can surface.

Building trust is a reciprocal process that calls upon you to enter into a professional relationship. As a racial equity leader, you trust that the educators are entering equity work, driven by the desire to do what is best for Black students. The educators, in turn, are trusting that you are not going to call them racists and blame them for Black student performance trends. Such reciprocal trust building not only enhances the professional relationship, but it positively affects student outcomes. "When educators trust their leaders and each other, academic achievement rises" (Saphier, 2018, para. 2). From the leader's lens, trusting those on the journey with you communicates your value and your belief in them (Modoono, 2017). Fostering trust is an essential component in creating spaces where educators commit to building their capacity, collaborating with their peers, and demonstrating the vulnerability needed to advance their ability to engage in anti-racist mindsets and behaviors.

Yet race and racism can breed distrust and undermine our attempts to forge authentic relationships. Understanding racism and the dynamics associated with building trust are equally vital to building a culture intent on changing the dynamics, experiences, and outcomes for Black students. Racial equity leaders must have patience and perseverance to build trust. The foundation for trust is established through

- **Active** engagement in the humanity of building relationships,

- **Exchanging** in professional conversations on education topics, and

- **Demonstrating** words and actions that align to beliefs in changing the outcomes for students of color.

Let us reference Ms. Tallador and her shared experiences from the beginning of the chapter to examine how being active, exchanging, and demonstrating may manifest in practice.

Active Engagement

Active engagement is demonstrated in the humanity of building relationships. It is imperative to play an active role that shows consideration and care for other people. Active engagement requires us to

- Be responsive when the educator is communicating,

- Be honest in interactions with the educator, and

- Honor confidentiality when asked not to disclose information to others. (Russell, 2016)

Our equity meetings make me feel . . . well . . . mostly uncomfortable, uncertain, and guilty. I am sure everyone notices how awkward these meetings are for me. In every other setting with my same colleagues, I am engaging, and talking is not an issue.

Ms. Tallador acknowledged that she engages and participates in other settings despite not engaging or sharing her voice in the equity meetings. In the meetings, where she is actively engaged and confident, she is likely speaking from her place of comfort. For the leader, this space of comfort and confidence is her entry point for engagement. When she is speaking and being responsive, you must actively listen to her. Listen for what she discusses, how she discusses it, and why it matters to her. When there are opportunities for one-on-one conversations, ask her questions related to her interests, the information from the conversations where you were an active listener, and the equity meetings. Be authentic and honest with your interactions to make connections and to discover or understand commonalities that you share.

Exchanging in Professional Conversations

Exchange in professional conversations on education and non-education topics. Exchanging in conversations allows the racial equity leader and educator to hear what is important to the other person. Discussion of non-education topics also enables further insight into the other person's interests and background experiences.

I struggle because I know I am more "woke" than most of my colleagues. I read books on race; I go to professional developments to better educate myself. I marched in a Black Lives Matter protest. I want this world to be a better place. Professional conversation related to work and topics outside of work may allow the leader to have a better understanding of Ms. Tallador's experiences, especially when the interest does not align with the behavior demonstrated. These interests may lend themselves to deeper conversations. Focusing only on work topics provides only one dimension of the person and may exclude the opportunities for deeper, more meaningful discourse.

Demonstrating With Words and Actions

Demonstrate with words and actions the belief in impacting outcomes for students of color. Consistency is key. A workshop cannot be the only space where the leader communicates the necessity and urgency of the work. Trust will not be established if words and actions in training do not match actual conversations and behaviors outside of the training.

(Continued)

(Continued)

Yet during the meetings, I sit in silence. I do not trust anyone enough to talk about my feelings or ask questions. I am conflicted because even when I know I should interrupt a racist discourse among colleagues, I do not. I smile, I nod, and I remain silent. Ms. Tallador's words are reflected in her actions of silence and disengagement. Your behavior cannot match Ms. Tallador's. Authentic engagement through conversation, modeling, and actions must be consistent in how you show up in your daily interactions. As the relationship builds with Ms. Tallador and the conversations deepen during your exchanges, there will be opportunities to create space for Ms. Tallador to ask questions or share her feelings without fear of blame or judgment. In those moments, the words and actions demonstrated by the leader may impact Ms. Tallador's level of vulnerability.

Pause and Reflect

While implementing the active, exchange, and demonstrate strategies to build trust, ask yourself these questions:

- How will you know that trust is being built?

- How do you monitor your progress?

- How does trust sound?

- How does trust look?

Journal Prompts

Stop and think about what's coming up for you regarding building trust with educators.

Reflect on the practices you have used to build trust in professional relationships.

Consider how a lack of building trust among educators on an equity journey may be a detriment to equity goals.

Ponder a world where there is open, honest dialogue and actions to eliminate the institutionalized racist practices driving the decision making for students of color.

Trust building requires time and commitment, which appears to conflict with the urgency for the change in outcomes for students of color. More, trust building and taking action to address the marginalization of Black and Brown students are not mutually exclusive. Trust building is a continuous process and will occur throughout the building of equity capacity among the team. The movement from dysconsciousness to consciousness, depicted in the CARE framework, will reflect varying levels of trust from those engaged at different points in the process.

Vulnerability in a Trusted Space

Vulnerability sounds like truth and feels like courage.
Truth and courage aren't always comfortable, but they're
never weakness.

Dr. Brené Brown

As previously stated, trust is the foundation for vulnerability. Without trust, educators are less likely to show the vulnerability that fuels personal introspection and the in-depth conversations that help us understand the lens of analysis needed for racial equity. Building trust requires us to listen and engage in conversations and follow-up conversations. These experiences enhance educators' willingness to be vulnerable. A characteristic of unhealthy culture is the negative mindset associated with vulnerability. For some, vulnerability evokes "weakness" or negative experiences. In these negative experiences, the act of demonstrating vulnerability was not received positively; nor was it reciprocated in the response or acknowledged by the other person(s). Vulnerability suggests risk—a potential for harm. Educators and leaders often work diligently to protect themselves by avoiding vulnerability or discussing topics that may expose their vulnerabilities. There is a pervasive mindset showing vulnerability, and "weakness" is like kryptonite to becoming a "super" educator.

The most effective way to counter such negative mindsets is to display our own vulnerability and reframe it as an essential step toward building our capacity to address racial inequities.

When educators share their vulnerabilities, they open the door to more in-depth individual and collective engagement. Inevitably, statements, beliefs, and dilemmas will surface that demand interruption. In such cases, first unpack what needs to be interrupted to promote greater understanding, reflection, and growth on the part of educators.

Building trust and creating space for people to share their vulnerabilities, especially on racialized topics, will elevate the educator's voice on rooted issues impacting Black students. The educators' voices also build and support a culture of sharing thoughts, practices, and experiences to address racial inequities. Consider the following "Questions to Reengage in Conversation" as a point of unpacking and questioning a racialized dynamic that requires interruption. The questions will guide your thinking as you prepare for an intentional "comeback" conversation or a follow-up discussion that allows purposeful direction and deeper processing of the dynamic with the person(s) involved.

Questions to Reengage in Conversation

- What was the situation, comment, or dynamic requiring engagement or reengagement?

- What needs to change with the situation, comment, or dynamic? How does the situation, comment, or dynamic relate to race and equity work?

- What do you know about the person? What have you learned about the person based on what was shared?

- How do race and intersectionality impact the situation?

- What are your outstanding questions? What are your questions to reengage the comeback conversation?

- What are your next steps and follow-up with the person? How will you engage and facilitate the comeback conversation?

The Questions to Reengage in Conversation allow reflection on the situation, comment, or dynamic and utilize the information gathered to be intentional in the reengagement. Some extraordinary leaders can and will be able to complete this reflection process in real time during the exchange with the educator. However, some exceptional leaders will utilize the reflection aspects of the process to deepen their questions and use coaching strategies to reengage for a more meaningful dialogue.

Although this is an intentional conversation, you are not stalking the educator, as that would diminish the level of trust you have worked so hard to build. Remember to enter the conversation with a focus to facilitate further exchange. More importantly, no one wants to talk to someone who is firing questions at them and taking notes on their responses. As the racial equity leader, be mindful of how you "show up." This is not a surprise attack, and the leader must use good judgment to read the situation and determine if the educator is in a space to engage in a conversation. If the timing is not appropriate, do not force the conversation. Another opportunity will present itself.

The CARE framework emphasizes how building trust and vulnerability are necessary components of community building. The exchange described in the "Interruptions" box would likely not have surfaced without some level of trust among community members. And, if the underlying belief systems are not fully exposed, how can we be expected to interrupt negative mindsets?

Interruptions

During an observation of a schoolwide data meeting, as the racial equity leader, you hear a veteran teacher share with a table of her peers.

"I don't know what they want or expect us to do. I think we should be celebrating given what students we had to teach. Those results are great for them. Since they want to talk about data, I had 28 students in my class. Of my 28 students, 14 were new this year due to the boundary change and arrived with very horrible grades. I guess that is why their school closed. Five of the 14 had behavioral issues from Day 1, and they

(Continued)

(Continued)

did nothing about them. Two of the five students with behavioral issues should have been expelled because they were so disrespectful and disruptive. They never did any work or paid any attention to me. These kids stopped my good kids from really learning. Yeah, but no one wants to talk about those data points."

Use the Questions to Reengage in Conversation to reflect, process, and create direction to reengage the educator in a comeback conversation.

Voices During the Journey

Great teams do not hold back with one another.

They are unafraid to air their dirty laundry. They admit their mistakes, their weaknesses, and their concerns without fear of reprisal.

Patrick Lencioni

Lencioni (2002) describes how trust and vulnerability can manifest into a great team. However, great teams usually do not start out great. They build their capacity to become high-functioning teams. Expect some turbulence along the path to building racial equity capacity across a team. When we establish a culture that embraces trust and vulnerability, expect to encounter statements and beliefs that may be deeply steeped in White supremacy. These include expressions of White privilege and White fragility, vestiges of White supremacy that typically offend and may be challenged by persons of color and some White people.

DiAngelo (2011) describes White fragility as a state where a minimum amount of racial stress challenges the comfort level of a White person, which creates a range of defensive actions inclusive of emotions, adverse reactions, or responses. Racial equity work may produce racial stress for White people. Centering on a person's race to contrast what has been established by the dominant White culture defies and confronts what is known, accepted, and familiar. Defying and confronting what is known, accepted, and familiar with race challenges the White dominant culture's authority, objectivity, historical perspective, and entitlement to comfort. For White people in support of racial equity, defying and confronting are a challenge to White solidarity. The defensive actions are often an attempt to reinstate what is racially familiar or comfortable. Given the dynamic of White fragility, race equity leaders should expect that feelings will be hurt; there may be anger, tears, and frustration. As demonstrated by Ms. Tallador, some staff members may be silent, while the racial equity leader may be experiencing some of the same feelings. Despite such challenges to cultures built on trust and vulnerability, these emotions are quite common and natural in the course of racial equity work. As voices become more transparent, more trusting, and frankly more honest, the likelihood of discord increases.

Reactive Versus Proactive

When a person has been harmed in the course of a relationship, restoration is needed for the relationship to continue. Professional relationships operate in the same manner. As a leader of equity, at some point during your journey, there will be conflict. You may encounter conflict among a group of educators on their journey, or your own internal conflict might emerge in your relationship with a member of your team. Your teammates will expect you to create conditions to resolve conflict. Unhealthy conflicts could be detrimental to a team if they continue without communication and restoration. There are times when healthy verbal engagements between adults present as conflict. The "Indicators of Healthy Conflict" may appear to be troubling but can lead to engagement at a deeper level for the community.

Indicators of Healthy Conflict

- Open processing or wrestling with concepts, thoughts, and ideas

- Questioning for understanding and curiosity

- Changing opinions or thoughts among members of the group

- Students needs are at the core of the work

(Aguilar, 2016)

As you build your community, you will need to learn how to discern the difference between healthy and unhealthy conflict among the team. Your goal is to be responsive. Sometimes those responses will be reactive. Being reactive, in this context, is to deal with conflicts after they emerge (Dinsmore, 1988). There will be times when the leader gains awareness through reacting and learning to be proactive for the next situation. It is better to be reactive and responsive than not to respond at all. Being proactive focuses on strategic thinking and acting before conflicts emerge (Dinsmore, 1988). Examples of how a racial equity leader can be proactive versus reactive include the following:

- Proactive leaders create conditions that allow for each person's voice and experience to be heard and elevated. Reactive leaders are not intentional in building community to create conditions to elevate each person's voices. In the opening vignette with Ms. Tallador, a reactive leader will recognize that Ms. Tallador is silent and not engaged. In an attempt to elevate her voice, a reactive leader may bring attention to her disengagement during the meeting. The leader needs to first consider and seek clarity to why Ms. Tallador is disengaging, but centering her fragility during the meeting will not have a positive impact on her trust and ability to be vulnerable within the space.

- Proactive leaders establish co-constructed norms for engagement. As noted in the previous chapter, the CARE framework provides an understanding of the need to establish a shared vocabulary to engage and communicate how and what educators are experiencing. Reactive leaders do not create conditions or co-constructed norms and protocols that allow for truth, transparency, and permission to be authentically engaged and be accountable. For example, Ms. Tallador may benefit from conversation protocols establishing the necessary vocabulary to better engage in race conversations.

- Proactive leaders consistently follow up with comeback conversations after shared experiences to allow additional processing and connecting. Reactive leaders are responsive in the training or meeting, but they do not engage in additional conversations. The racial equity journey is often contained to the professional development with little to no application outside of the meeting or training. Ms. Tallador's shared experiences should facilitate a comeback conversation to unpack and process her experiences. Utilizing the CARE framework, these comeback conversations with Ms. Tallador would meet her individually where she is on the continuum of awareness and begin her equity journey to engendering awareness with goals of co-constructing knowledge to apply.

Aguilar (2016) articulates three key strategies when managing unhealthy conflict:

- Name the conflict.

- Address the conflict now or later.

- Anchor team members in the established norm.

Naming the conflict means that you acknowledge there is a conflict, and you identify what it is. Earlier in the chapter, we underscored the importance of eliminating a culture of blame; naming a conflict does not mean you blame those involved in the conflict. Blaming often leads to defensive responses and a breakdown in communication. A conflict that leads to a communication breakdown will impact how the educators interact with each other and, subsequently, how you interact with them individually and collectively. When communication stops, especially between people of color and White people, the equity work stalls, and the potential for a toxic culture begins to form. There will be times when you will have to decide if you will address the conflict in the moment or later. Managing the conflict can range from acknowledging the discomfort and having a comeback conversation to facilitating a restorative meeting between two people or a group of people. When we act proactively by co-constructing norms or consensus regarding how adults will engage with each other, we can diminish the possibility of communication breakdowns. We must call out or interrupt when those co-constructed norms are ignored by respectfully reminding the team of the agreed-to norm and the rationale for the co-constructed norm. For example, if an established norm is following a protocol for discussions to respect the voices and perspective of all members of the team and adults are not adhering to the co-constructed norm, racial equity leaders might respond as follows:

1. **Identify the cause for interruption:** *Team, just a reminder to remember our established norms of using our protocol when responding and speaking.*

2. **Communicate the impact and consequences of ignoring the co-constructed norm:** *Using our protocol allows all members of our team to engage and share their insights.*

Notice that avoiding the conflict was not an option.

Restoration Versus Disconnection

Unhealthy conflicts can sometimes cause people, including the racial equity leader, to retreat. You are leading, but you are also rooted in the experience as you are leading. You are in the collective, which means you are also immersed in the work, and you may experience the same spectrum of feelings as those you are leading. Disconnection (self-imposed or group constructed) of the members from the equity work is not an option. To proactively address possible disconnection from the equity journey in response to an unhealthy conflict, cultivate a therapeutic mindset to restore relationships among the team members. Time and energy must be dedicated to restorative approaches with adults to uplift the community. We not only strive to preserve community to promote equity outcomes; we also need to remember that while we work to center our students, we also address our uniquely human attributes, including how we value each other while building agency.

According to Morrison and Vaandering (2012), the premise of restorative practices was to address the imbalance between power and status. The researchers argued leaders must advance the power of relationship building and understanding over the power of the institution to punish. Although the concept of restorative practices is being utilized to address years of systemic racist practices against students of color, the concept and guiding principles are centered on the human when working with educators to build their equity capacity.

The goal of incorporating restorative measures within your practice is to provide opportunities for members of the community to have ownership and responsibility for their behavior without being isolated from the community. Let us think back to our reactive leader, who recognized that Ms. Tallador was silent and not engaged during the equity meetings. While attempting to elevate Ms. Tallador's voice, the reactive leader centered attention to her disengagement during the meeting. Ms. Tallador felt misunderstood entirely and began to find ways to avoid the meetings, the leader, and the equity work.

Leaders cannot build a community if they are continually losing or removing members. The reactive leader in Ms. Tallador's situation must respond to Ms. Tallador's isolation from the community by engaging her in a comeback conversation. The leader would use the Questions to Reengage in Conversations to allow reflection and introspection into the situation with Ms. Tallador, reflecting on comments made and any other information shared to be intentional in the restorative conversation that must occur.

In the dynamic with Ms. Tallador, the conversation's goal would be for the leader to be accountable for their behaviors, reestablish communication with Ms. Tallador, and potentially engage in conversation related to the situation resulting in isolation. Active listening is necessary from the leader. Being intentional in your restorative approaches fosters a community that values relationships and strives for a level of compassion that supports building educators' equity capacity rather than defeating people while building their capacity. The latter will derail your equity goals and, subsequently, the necessary outcomes for students of color. As a racial equity leader, knowing the worth of community building will help build capacity and strengthen your capacity as a racial equity leader.

What Nobody Talks About

Often people of color are problematized because those with power and position are not willing to remove the practices and policies steeped in racism that are created, implemented, and followed.

Your Lived Experience

Your lived experiences shape your reality.

- How will your experiences, especially related to race and racism, impact or guide your work in and with the community?

- Using your sphere of influence as the center, what are the racial nuances of your community?

- What are your commitments to elevating an anti-racist culture in the work and learning environment?

Chapter Reflection

- What are the dual roles that must be honored by the racial equity leader? Why are those roles important to community building?

- How will you facilitate the action of building trust?

- How do you maintain community during conflict? Why is it necessary to name conflict when it occurs?

Part II

Leaning Into the Learning - The Making Meaning Space

Power and Influence

4

//

In Chapter 3, we examined the role of trust in advancing equity leadership in an organization. As practitioners, we know that this is often an unexamined condition that has significant impact on an organization's capacity for navigating interpersonal dynamics that influence progress toward anti-racist functioning. As you consider evidence of trust within the relationships in your organization, you must also examine the organization's nexus of power. This chapter will deepen your contemplative engagement in the assessment of organizational culture by naming and examining power.

In the summer of 2020, the world was on fire contending with issues of race and racism across the globe. Far from the fringe, Black Lives Matter as a mantra and a movement seemed a place of respite from the continuous bombardment of racial trauma. Students, schools, and school districts were not excluded from the impact of such a profoundly racialized moment. Student protests and demands prompted organizations' responses around the country: Do Black lives matter? That is the question that was asked of district leadership all over the country. Both Dr. Willis, a White male superintendent, and Dr. McCall, a Black female superintendent, respond affirmatively to calls from students and the community to support Black Lives Matter. Each released eloquent statements affirming support for Black lives, eschewing racism and institutional violence, and committing to the work of advancing race equity within their districts. Dr. Willis is viewed as a hero. A White male leader using his power and privilege to support historically marginalized communities. A social justice warrior. The response to Dr. McCall is decidedly different. She is called divisive. Her community accuses her of caring only for Black students. They go as far as to state that their district does not have those issues. Dr. McCall is now fighting for her job in a moment when a global pandemic is disproportionately affecting communities of color, specifically the Black community; there have been almost monthly incidents of extra-judicial killings of Black men and women in encounters with police. How is this happening when both of these individuals have significant authority by virtue of their positions? Both have long careers of serving diverse bodies of student, faculty, and communities well. Why is a Black woman's support of Black lives radical while a White male doing the same is not?

Pause and Reflect

What are the things you need to consider as you intersect your racial identity with your organizational positioning?

How do you identify allies that help you to advance a position of racial justice for your organization?

These questions are bound in the power proposition embedded in the racial construction. As a prelude to diving into your study of power, we suggest beginning with the following framing from the renowned attorney and scholar, Kimberlé Crenshaw (2017, para. 5):

> Intersectionality is a lens through which you can see where power comes and collides, where it interlocks and intersects. It is not simply that there is a race problem here, a gender problem here, and a class or LBGTQ [sic] problem there. Many times, that framework erases what happens to people who are subject to all of these things.

As you unpack this idea of intersectionality, you will likely begin to have a heightened understanding of why the communities have different expectations for Dr. Willis and Dr. McCall. What is it about Dr. Willis's maleness that gives him a particular social standing that Dr. McCall's femaleness does not? Both are seasoned administrators; however, Dr. Willis is able to stand in solidarity with his Black and Brown students. When Dr. McCall communicates her affirmation of Black Lives Matter, she is not only questioned, but she is also characterized as engaging in illegal, partisan activity. How do Blackness and Whiteness influence these dynamics? Even when power is presumed, as is the case with our two sitting district superintendents, the interplay of race and gender reveals an unjust social arrangement. We submit, those aspiring to leadership for transformational change need to understand these dynamics.

The Social Arrangement We Live With

We are inhabiting a rare moment in time: After so many years of silence and subterfuge, numerous high-profile Americans, including President Biden, have publicly stated that dismantling systemic racism must be made a national priority. Thanks to our enhanced ability to capture and transmit video footage with our mobile devices, the realities of "living while Black," such as Amy Cooper's frantic phone call to the NYPD after encountering a Black male birdwatcher in Central Park, have made the national news. Such shameful spectacles, coupled with the televised 2020 murder of George Floyd, and the murder of Breonna Taylor, have served to highlight the need to cultivate anti-racist spaces. In response to this global breaking point, many public, private, and non-profit institutions have adjusted their annual budget allocations to identify fiscal resources for "racial equity training." In the same spirit, we are witnessing a surge of appointments of chiefs of equity and diversity across various organizations. Such responses may appear, on the surface, as a breath of fresh air since organization leaders and boards are professing a commitment to eliminate institutional racism. However, without a plan for institutional transformation, creating positions, departments, or workshops is insufficient to interrupt oppressive conditions. What we know about racism (and other systems of oppression) is that they are adaptive and can morph in ways that simple solutions fail to address. It is absolutely possible, as a result, to achieve the goal of racial diversity in hiring (for example) within an organization without interrupting racism within said organization.

Interruptions

Don't accept transactions where transformed systems are required. Transactions and transformations are not synonymous.

The fundamental issue related to structural racism is the power dynamic (and its unequal distribution). According to the Aspen Institute and the Applied Research Institute at Berkeley (Lawrence & Keleher, 2004), structural racism is "the normalization and legitimization of an array of dynamics—historical, cultural, institutional and interpersonal—that routinely advantage Whites while producing cumulative and chronic adverse outcomes for people of color" (p. 1). Using this definition, we argue that leading with a justice-centered framework of accountability is essential in the work of dismantling institutional racism. We have learned through our professional and lived experience that relegating "equity work" to the efforts of a single individual or department will do little to dismantle the structural racism that is the root cause of the problem. Anti-racist leadership requires nothing less than a commitment to applying the lens of anti-oppression—a lens that problematizes all forms of structural inequality—where outcomes are more important than intent.

Journal Prompt

Critique your experience within your organization as it relates to race equity/anti-racism work, using the context above. How would you describe its response?

Figure 4.1   Conscious Anti-Racist Engendering (CARE) Framework

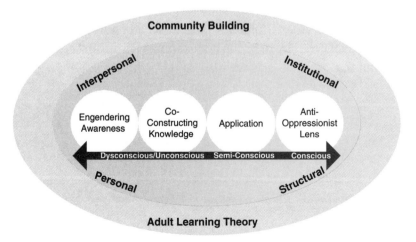

It is critical that engaging the task of dismantling systems of oppression is done using a strategic lens of engagement. This means that it is crucial that strategic planning is used as the organization advances anti-oppression across the organization. Typically, most organizations in the early stages of engaging in intersectional racial equity work must tackle a myriad of interlocking issues that have perpetuated marginalizing conditions. Let's refer to the conscious anti-racist engendering (CARE) framework (Figure 4.1 on the facing page), as we work through some reflection points on our journey toward structural transformation.

Honoring Humanity in Our Communities

Recall that the model begins with the essential work of building community. We honor humanity and authentic relationships first and foremost in building communities that work to dislodge inequity.

Co-Constructing Knowledge

How are dominant ways of knowing de-centered so that marginalized ways of knowing can gain power? In addressing this question, we might interrogate ideas like how the organizational culture "best" operates, what constitutes "best" practice, processes used to make decisions, and so forth. We not only co-construct new knowledge but we engage in practice, drawing from our co-constructed knowledge, with the goal of replacing entrenched, Eurocentric ways of being with those that are anti-racist. Through our conversations, engagement, and continuous efforts to raise our racial consciousness, we institutionalize our collective learning rooted in anti-racism (and other efforts to address intersecting forms of structural inequity). Ultimately, we transform our organizations. This interplay between personal and organizational change is an ongoing iterative process. It is not just the organization that is different, but the individuals who form the organization are different as well.

A Purposeful Disinvestment in "Rugged Individualism"

In work situations, our norm is to engage in transactional relationships, that is, relationships that exist for the sole purpose of completing tasks. Such relationships fall short in supporting the depth of "knowing" that is required to honor humanity. Part of the purported ethos of the American idea is that individuals succeed by the "sweat of their brow." The Horatio Algiers mythology of every man pulling himself up by his "bootstraps" is in many ways implicitly and explicitly proffered as a norm. There are many consequences of such mythology, but as it relates to doing the work of organizational transformation, the proposition dooms efforts. First, it centers the perspective of the person with authority-based power as the central way of knowing, being, and conceptualizing. Second, it devalues the community-driven nature of organizational transformation that centers justice.

In communities where relationships are created through transactions, harm happens, microaggressions are normalized, and certain bodies are invisibilized. This way of being emerges as the standard form of interaction within an organization; in essence, it becomes the organizational culture. Our cultural counternarrative, the beloved community discussed earlier in this book, is best be described in the writings of Dr. Martin Luther King Jr. He describes this community as "a society based on justice, equal opportunity, and love of one's fellow human beings." Communities that center justice in a society structured on inequity require deliberate efforts and collective responsibility, beginning with continuous critical reflection on our own epistemologies. Such reflection is prompted with the following questions:

1. How do I know what I know?

2. Am I willing to examine the essence of the truths I hold?

To move ourselves and our organizations closer to institutionalizing an anti-racist culture, the community commits to learning that involves surfacing, naming, uncovering, interrogating, and healing so that not only does the organization function differently but its people are indeed different. This transformation occurs through a non-linear personal journey that intersects at various learning moments within the organization. The CARE framework taps into our collective ability to gauge progress within the institution.

Pause and Reflect

Think about the last decision made in your office, school, department, and/or organization? Who made the decision? What was the impact? Were those affected most by the decision at the table participating in the decision-making process?

As examples, consider a police officer walking hand-in-hand with protestors at a Black Lives Matter rally; a football franchise owner leaving his owner's box to kneel in solidarity with some of players during the national anthem; or teachers petitioning their school boards to de-center Whiteness in the curriculums. Each anti-racist action, though experienced and nuanced differently, demonstrates a different level of coming into consciousness that is part of the journey. Rather than problematize development, our model invites the community to engage in open dialogue. These are conversations where outcomes can be assessed, intentions can be examined, and framing can be interrogated. We proffer that multifaceted engagements grounded in integrated learning are essential conditions for an organization to build capacity to dismantle structural racism. The CARE framework is constructed to help practitioners understand these theoretical underpinnings.

Pause and Reflect

When you hold a staff meeting with multiple agenda items, consider how an individual might be personally dysconscious and semi-conscious at different moments during the same meeting depending on the topic discussed. How might the CARE framework assist a meeting facilitator with surfacing the issue and then engendering awareness and co-constructing knowledge as a community? If it would be helpful during this reflective exercise, use the police officer who participated in a Black Lives Matter protest as an example. For context, the pictures from the protest were all over the news. In the spirit of honoring the humanity of all individuals, how might CARE framework assist the commanding officer when the topic is discussed at an upcoming patrol meeting?

Power Is Complex and Issues of Racial Equity and Anti-Racism Are Always About Power

Power is an elusive idea. Power has the ability to be ever present and invisible at the same time. Those who have outsized power often make (what they deem to be) small decisions that have major impacts on the lives of those with less power. Those with little power often exist under the burden of oppression to such a labored degree that they cannot imagine their lives could possibly work out in a different way. Power is a critical construct, which must be understood and interrogated if we are ever to dismantle systems of oppression in social organizations.

The Role of Power in Advancing the Race Equity Agenda

Challenges related to racial equity and access are fundamentally issues of power. The existence of structural racial inequities limit opportunities that can shape life outcomes. From before birth to death and beyond, race matters. From education, to health care, to access to healthy foods, to adequate housing, race matters. In addition, because race matters in all these ways and more, it is a liability to a healthy society to not understand its phenomenology and the mechanisms that make it so predictive across the lifespan. We contend that this understanding needs to begin with recognizing that it is not enough to just speak truth to power but also to speak about the nature of power (which in a racialized context means examining White cultural dominance). This responsibility belongs to everyone and is essential to our goal of restoring our collective humanity.

In a society that values White skin, White frames of knowing and experiencing the world are essential survival skills. If this sounds too abstract to you, try to imagine yourself as a Black male in an overpoliced neighborhood where knowing how to navigate police interactions could make the difference between making it home or not. Similarly, try to imagine what it is like to learn in a Eurocentric curriculum context where you cannot see either yourself or your life reflected. In school, the understanding is that one's "hard work" is sufficient to succeed is a startling contrast to a non-White student's exposure to structures that are implicitly and explicitly positioned to undervalue and erase their existence. In this scenario, simply graduating is an accomplishment. In another example, figuring out how to accumulate and pass generational wealth to your child when you hail from a community that has been de facto and de jure estranged from the financial mainstream of the richest country in the world is the story of genius in its elegant complexity. These are but a few manifestations of the barriers that Black people in particular and people of color, in general, navigate moment by moment in a society that does not equally value all of its citizens.

While persons of color face the daunting task of navigating such complexities, they must simultaneously contend with the harsh reality that non-White ways of knowing, being, and ultimately investing are undervalued in our society. All the more reason that our beloved community must also contend with these realities. We do so through both a reconceptualization and a reconfiguration of how systems of oppression function. This is a statement of the nature of power that we submit should be understood.

Many of the common organizational responses to revelations of the need for anti-racism/anti-oppression work (i.e., technical solutions) do not deal with the wide range of dimensions that the historical web of racial barriers created. Without analysis rooted in an anti-racist/ anti-oppressionist lens, organization leaders simply repackage ideas steeped in White racially dominant ways of being and understanding that serve to maintain the status quo. Acts of "organizational performative wokeness" can be potentially devastating for staff who live in bodies that are targets of structural racism. This reality of the value proposition with which different groups are treated is fundamental to issues of equity in general and race equity in particular. Social service institutions, like schools, have both a historical and a determinative role in either perpetuating or interrupting racial injustice.

Pause and Reflect

Consider how students of color, generally, and Black students, specifically, often experience classrooms that do not value their contributions, that fail to include opportunities for them to see their genius as center to the curriculum and not added as a supplementary lesson or unit. In the alternative, consider how individuals of color, generally, and Black individuals, specifically, experience your organization. How are they seeing themselves as integral *or not* to the work within the organization?

Within your school, business, or non-profit organization, are the voices of non-White groups heard? How do you know? How are those voices used to drive the organization's vision setting? How do you know? Does your organization's outputs/outcome data align with the organization's vision?

Naming Power and Influence

Positional, relational, and expertise-based are three types of power within most organizations. As you identify the power dynamic within your organization, consider how the power is derived. *Positional power* is garnered mostly from an individual's formal position or title. Although it is the most easily identified type of power, it is also the most normalized. Position does not have inherent guarantees of empathy, wisdom regarding differences in lived experience, or knowledge of how systems of oppression operate. This is what makes the construct of power imbalance rooted in positions especially dangerous to organizations seeking to dismantle systems of oppression. We argue that those with a great degree of power rooted in position have an especially important responsibility for personal introspection and accountability in organizations seeking to dismantle structural racism.

Relational power is the chief agency within many organizations. This type of power, when coupled with the transformative work of creating more inclusive environments, can be the primary driver of anti-racist work within an organization. In particular, people working together, lending support, problem solving, and organizing are likely the unspoken heartbeats within organizations. When these relationships are constructed on equality, shared vision and purpose, and collective accountability for impact over intent, they can serve as the embodiment of the aspirations of the organization. Therefore, identifying relational powers requires a comprehensive understanding of the internal operations of an organization.

Expertise-based power is the power associated with an individual's deep and/or unique skills, knowledge, and competencies. Here again, this model of power distribution can be deeply problematic with organizations designed to serve human beings. Valuing and devaluing staff based on the knowledge they hold is an implicit precept in organizations that prize content in these ways. Organizations designed to support people need to intentionally design to value people! It doesn't matter if we are experts in the planning and delivery of online learning during a global pandemic if we don't similarly have a deep understanding of the real-life disruptions and trauma that children and families are experiencing as a result of the pandemic. It doesn't matter if we can fundraise a surplus budget for our non-profit annually if our giving mechanism crowds out the very people positioned to advance the mission of the organization. We would offer that in most cases, the very definition of "expert" is a problematic construct within most organizations. Given the dynamic of organizations, the power interplay, when examined closely, can be named.

We maintain it is essential to analyze the ways in which power is used to maintain structures that underserve people of color.

Ideas to Sit With

On which type of power are you expending most of your energy?

What are the consequences of this expenditure?

When your ability to engage in a sharp power dynamic analysis is enhanced, you can also begin to evaluate the impact of influence within any organization or situation. Consider the Black parent who is able to identify the "othering" of her child in kindergarten. Her child, her beautiful Black son, is innocent and deserved to have his experience validated, honored, and uplifted in the instructional design, the classroom culture, student-to-student interactions, and the teacher-student interactions. During conversations with her son, coupled with classroom observations, this Black parent identified multiple examples that created a pattern of exclusion. Unambiguously, this parent identified multiple instances that resulted in her son being excluded from play opportunities. Moreover, she was told that her son exhibited problematic behavior, although other young, White students who were engaged in the same behavior in the same set of circumstances, were never called out. Further, the kindergarten teacher described her son as lacking early learning experiences even though he had been enrolled in a prominent local early center since 2 years of age. Initially, the Black parent felt she did not have any power to address the issue. However, she had tremendous influence. Her ability to mobilize other Black parents by writing letters to the school principal, central office staff, superintendent, and school board members was utilized. Further, she wrote an op-ed letter to the local newspaper, and her collective actions grabbed the attention of other like-minded Black parents to form the first Black Parents Action Group in her child's school district. As a result of this mobilization, the group is now invited to meet quarterly with the superintendent, as well as invited to speak monthly at the school board meeting with other board-recognized stakeholder groups. Cultivating an understanding of the command of influence is essential to authentic engagement in this work.

Where to Start

As previously stated, examining the dynamics of dominant and sub-ordinate positioning and how such positioning perpetuates injustice will further our community's goal of providing opportunities for all of its members. When such power-driven relationships and their accompanying consequences are experienced and perceived by most as normal and natural, our logical starting point is to question the meaning of "normal and natural." This surfacing or *seeing* is an essential antecedent to disruption. We will quickly find that such Eurocentric ways of being and experiencing the world are endemic to our collective socialization in both overt obvious ways and nuanced subtle ones. These Eurocentric ideas are normalized in the environment of the culture of the organizations. Examples include common things such as the assumptions that are made about the patterns of and the "hard work" of the employee or lack thereof, the idea that busy-ness means effectiveness, or lack of credence given to experiences that are not documented. We argue that there are common ideological and material manifestations of these power dynamics, and to transform our organizations we must disrupt the dynamic.

This brings us back to the assertion that organizations seeking to engage a racial equity/anti-racism agenda must begin by creating a community that normalizes adult learning while cultivating critical consciousness. Additionally, these communities need to commit to authenticity and relationships and de-centering comfort and racially dominant ways of being and knowing. These are the preconditions to establish communities that could hold space for doing this work over the long term. Adult learning and authenticity are critical because the daily unconscious interpersonal racial dynamic we engage in are the building blocks of structural/institutional racism. That the perceptions, beliefs, and experiences of people of color in general and Black people in particular are undervalued and dismissed maintains the functioning of institutions as oppressive structures. That implicit and explicit lack of care or belief in the ability of non-White communities characterizes how we invest and dis-invest in them is foundational behavior in maintaining the problem. That there is deemed to be no or little wisdom in the ways of being people in unprotected bodies allows there to be no loss when decisions affecting us are made without us.

Pause and Reflect

Using the CARE framework, where are you in your racial awareness?

Have you reflected on the racial consciousness of your organization? Based on your reflection, what would you need to know to determine an entry point to engendering awareness?

Using the CARE framework, is there an opportunity to create multiple entry points for staff in the organization to assess the awareness aspect of your development plan (re: remember non-linear personal development continuum)?

Moving Into the Work of Creating Anti-Racist Organizations

Creating anti-racist organizations requires vigilance and vision, undergirded by moral clarity, in a society that normalizes marginalization. This is not a simple task. When we engage in surface-level racial equity work but fail to question our organizational (and societal) norms, the organization remains unchanged in its character even as some of its outward-facing artifacts seem different. There is a difference between "improving" conditions and "transforming" conditions.

Interruptions

Be impeccable with your language. Differentiate where improvements versus transformations are needed!

In far too many cases, as organizations seek to do racial equity work with the aim of developing anti-racist functioning, the changes that are the most important are those that the organization has the least conscious awareness of. Caustic power dynamics are typically unnamed, unexamined, and normalized. Admittedly, interrogating the nature of power and surfacing disturbing truths will not be easy. The nature of power is that it can define (in very self-reinforcing ways) the essence of what is real and what is not. The nature of power can delineate what is normal and what is abnormal. The nature of power is that in extreme cases, it can determine that rain was falling on a clear bright sunny day. Moreover, to varying degrees, we have all been socialized to accept "truth" in this way. We contend that while an organizational champion/champions are necessary, training provided in a context of learning and visionary leadership are essential components; a commitment to not just "doing different" but "being different" is essential.

So What, Now What?

Understanding the nature of power can be a traumatic experience in a community, particularly for those who have suffered abuses. Healing and repairing are critical considerations as organizations seek to advance an anti-racist agenda. It is equally important that the community shares a willingness to be transformed. Community agreement is required. This agreement should state that when offered new information, different perspectives, and new revelations, all will lean into co-constructing a different reality. This is the journey members are willing to take.

A data-informed process that values stories and experiences in ways we know to value numbers and other measures are important. Strategic planning that allows transparent recursive ways to close the gaps between rhetoric and behavior is crucial. This complex work cannot be accomplished by simply offering equity training alone and/or hiring one person to "lead" equity work for your entire organization. Hence, technical solutions, while a part of this work, are not sufficient to get us to the place where organizations can functionally use an anti-oppression framing. The process of being anti-racist in ways of knowing and doing is an adaptive challenge that requires inclusivity. We hope that organizations choose transformation as this moment is so full of opportunity.

What Nobody Talks About

Racial equity is not what you do, it's who you are. It's not possible to create anti-racist organizations with people not committed to anti-racism. Power needs to be distributed within organizations seeking to be anti-racist.

Your Lived Experience

It is critical that as you "lead" this work, you are doing the work.

- How is your interrogation and examination of your identity informing how you advance the work in your organization?

- What have you learned about structural inequalities that have shaped your values?

- What is the evidence (your personal accountability) that your anti-racist values are shaping your living and leading?

Chapter Reflection

- Using the opening scenario of the two district superintendents, how might the two leverage the CARE framework in addressing the outrage associated with the Black Lives Matter declarative statement?

- Explain how you see power unfolding in your organization. Attempt to identify the power dynamics with respect to who is sitting where in the organization.

- Where do you think you can start to disrupt the power dynamics within your organization?

- Take a moment to reflect on your current role (as teacher, support staff, administrator, business leader, non-profit leader, etc.). Who is your main stakeholder group? How do you serve this stakeholder group? How are you using your influence to disrupt systems of oppressions, however small or big?

Invisibility and Other Barriers to Engaging in the Work of Anti-Racism and Structural Transformation

5

> *I am invisible, understand, simply because people refuse to see me.*
>
> *Ralph Ellison,* The Invisible Man

During a Monday staff meeting, packed with agenda items for discussion, Damita Miller sat quietly fuming. She was a third-year assistant principal at a middle school in a suburban school district. One of her daily assignments was to monitor seventh-grade lunch. Monday through Friday she spent from 12:15 to 1:05 pm with 350 energetic students at lunch. She would watch them choose seat mates, go to the vending machine for snacks, occasionally "jone on" one another, laugh out loud (really loud) at things she found only moderately funny, but this was lunchtime. She wanted students to have this brief moment to just be. The school was racially, ethnically, and socio-economically diverse. Most of the students were non-White, the majority Black, but White students were also a sizeable population. Among the White students, about 10% were Hispanic. Only 20% of students were not participating in free or reduced meals.

In making her rounds, checking in with each table of students, Damita was invited into an unanticipated discussion. "Young people, how is your day going?" she would ask. The response was normally "Good, Ms. Miller." But today, when she asked that question, Juanita, a really bubbly student leader, said she was having a horrible day. Damita asked if she wanted to talk about it. Juanita mumbled, "I'm sick of this. No one is doing anything about this." Now Damita was really curious: Who was no one, and what were they not doing? She wanted to know what had Juanita so bothered. Ms. Miller asked Juanita to step away from the group to talk. Juanita reluctantly agreed, but she seemed resigned. Ms. Miller said, "I honestly don't know what you are referring to. What's happening?" Juanita said, "I am one of three Black students in GT [gifted and talented] algebra. One of three. The teacher split us up, so I'm always in groups where I feel like I'm the only one. In the groups, every time I try to answer a question, I feel like I'm being dismissed. Like my ideas aren't good. I have had several conversations about group work with my teacher because she expects us to do most of our work that way. When I shared my experience, she told me I was being sensitive, and it is my responsibility to 'make people' hear me. When I've tried to do that, I get called angry and disruptive to the group. We spend half of the class period in group work every day. This means I have to deal with this every day, and I'm just tired of it. I'm going to ask my parents to move me into standard math. More of my friends are there, and I bet I won't have to fight like this every day." Ms. Miller said to Juanita that she was sorry she was experiencing this but asked if they could work on a plan to keep her in the class. Juanita said she would think about it but that if things didn't change, she would request a different class. As Damita Miller sat in the staff meeting, discussing new curriculum, observation schedules, extra duty assignments, and other topics, a thought kept recurring to her: "None of these things matter if any of our students are experiencing what Juanita is dealing with on a daily basis, and what's worse, in all the conversations we are having in this meeting, none come close to acknowledging this problem."

Pause and Reflect

Do you see yourself or your organization in Ms. Miller's story? If yes, how?

You Can't Solve a Problem That You Can't See

The nature of systems of dominance and oppression is that they get normalized and naturalized in a society. That which is perceived as normal and natural in a society is unremarkable. They are the stuff of "non-issues." They are the quintessential foundations of "that's just the way it is." But these are the very ideas that must be examined in organizations that seek to engage in transformative work. Additionally, the condition of invisibility, (i.e., what Juanita experienced in our opening story) in all its manifestations (values, beliefs, ideas, assumptions, people, and process) need to be named, surfaced, and examined. Culture, the everyday circumstances we work in, live in, and love in are like air—they are everywhere and nowhere at the same time.

The Conscious Anti-Racist Engendering (CARE) Framework

Ms. Miller's experience in the lunchroom illustrates the context that must be illuminated as our community sets out to interrupt common patterns of racial unconsciousness and dysconsciousness. The conscious anti-racist engendering (CARE) framework is the structure we use to describe both the theory and the process for ushering organizations through the process of de-institutionalizing structural racism and its intersections.

Figure 5.1 Conscious Anti-Racist Engendering (CARE) Framework

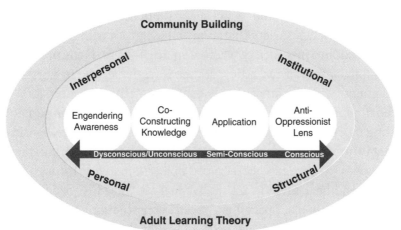

Engendering Awareness: Examining Identity in the Context of the Personal and Interpersonal

This chapter opens with a familiar scenario that often gets shared within the race equity practitioners' space. Racial harassment and isolation are happening in the organization. It is "subtle" until it's not. It is daily. It is reported. It is not the elephant in the room; it's the furniture in the room. Unfortunately, the response is often to dismiss, marginalize, or trivialize its existence. When Black or Brown children experience racial harassment, too often adults in positions of power will say, "Well, they call one another 'n—' so what difference does it make that other children use that language?" For those readers who find it difficult to believe that such statements are real, consider the following statistic. In 2019, the Southern Poverty Law Center published a report titled "Hate in Schools" (Costello & Dillard, 2019). Its findings among those interviewed showed that, two-thirds reported witnessing an issue of hate or bias in school. Further, the report found that "racism appears to be the motivation behind most hate and bias incidents in school, accounting for 63 percent of incidents reported in the news and 33 percent of incidents reported by teachers" (Costello & Dillard, 2019, p. 5). So how can a phenomenon be both present and invisible simultaneously? While the question seems like a riddle, it is one worth examining in the context of your lived experience, as well as, in your organization.

Very often, staff within an organization have not considered different aspects of their identity, and they are encouraged to "see people, not color." We are formally educated in schools that universalize learning conditions, content, and assessments of progress, all in service of notions of "equality" and "equal access." But herein lies the problem: We don't live in a society that treats all identities with equal access. We do not live in a society where we have universal interpretations of similar experiences. Said another way, the failure to nurture a community in a manner that encourages a critical examination of the fundamental inequalities of our society is a recipe for perpetuating if not exacerbating these inequalities. To dive deeper, consider that we are socialized in a society that is constantly delivering "raced messages." We see race stereotyped images constantly through television and hear them in music. We learn a "raced" version of U.S. history in schools. Space has "raced" constructions as evidenced by law enforcement engagement on bodies that seem to be "in the wrong place." These are just a few examples. That we don't encourage staff to examine ideas of race (and other intersecting identities) only makes them vulnerable to internalize messages and ways of being that stabilize systems of oppression.

Ideas to Sit With

Where does colorblindness show up in the organization? How can you begin the work to de-center it?

As an example, in a recent talk Isabel Wilkerson gave describing a central idea in her book *Caste*, she is quoted as stating, "In the fields of the Jim Crow south were opera singers, architects, engineers, etc. . . ." Try the following thought experiment:

1. Visualize Hispanic migrant workers, Black female certified nurse's aides, and disabled grocery store attendants.

2. Now visualize these same individuals as Fortune 500 CEOs, creators of new technologies that advance our world, or education leaders who run school systems through a realized lens of inclusion.

Not so easy, is it? The barrage of "raced messages" we have received throughout our lifetimes prevent many of us from envisioning these individuals in their new roles. Next, consider the consequences of this activity. How might the barriers you encountered during this activity be a reflection of your belief systems? How might such deficit belief systems also block or limit the professional opportunities available to these individuals (and many more not named)? Such are the consequences of ignoring how we have constructed our own identities and our thoughts and beliefs about the identity of others. By now, it should be clear that "colorblindness" is anything but that. Perpetuating the myth of colorblindness means perpetuating conditions in which White racial hegemony is unquestionably allowed to bestow benefits for its actors and exact significant penalty for those who deviate. This dangerous equation is enacted too often on a day-to-day, moment-to-moment basis, even while staff is simultaneously engaging in "equity discussions."

Personal Identity Development—You Get to Choose Your Racial Expression

As a race equity consultant, one of the most essential ideas to the necessity of raising aspects of internalized identity to the level of consciousness is the choice that can happen in that space. Race, gender, and class are socially constructed ideas in a society. Although these constructions are certainly meaningful in that beliefs and values of the dominant get codified in the policies, practices, and procedures that govern the function of organizations, it is also true that they often govern our personal decision making and dictate the terms of our interpersonal interactions. In the context of schooling, consider the complexity of inequitable access to rigorous courses like Gifted and Talented programs, STEM programs, or Advanced Placement. We have the structural issue that these opportunities are almost exclusively formed through Eurocentric ways of being and understanding the world. This organizational construction intuitively creates advantage for some and disadvantage for others in racially predictable ways. Let's assume an organization has some level of capacity to analyze these offerings through a "race equity lens" (a series of questions that center race in understanding the functioning of a given structure). We argue that although it is necessary to have capacity for this analysis, we must primarily be able to see our role in upholding these structures. In other words, to dismantle structures that uphold oppression, individuals need to have critical consciousness of how they have internalized dominant ideology. Further, individuals also need to do the internal work where they divest of this investment and decide how they will embody anti-oppressive ways of being, engaging, and leading. Said a different way, as we develop critical consciousness of dominance (in its many manifestations), we need to also decide who our persona of "resistance" will be. How does a doer of the work use their voice? How does a doer of the work use their power? How does a doer of the work use their silence? How do they disrupt? How do they conspire? These are the types of identity-based decisions that you need to make as you construct an identity that is a threat to structural oppression.

This is critically important because an organization cannot function differently (in a manner that centers racial equity) while its staff is unchanged. A foundational question that people working within a community desirous of a racially equitable environment must examine is, "How have I both internalized and manifested Eurocentric hegemonic ideas?"

Notice that we are not saying White people need to ask these questions, although unquestionably they do; we are saying that *people* need to ask these questions. *Through the process of examination and analysis of how I have constructed my identity through race, gender, class, and other socially constructed categories, I become a part of the change that the collective is pursuing at the organizational level. Through my willful and deliberate examination of messaging that I've internalized over the course of my life, from family, school, media, the behaviors that were affirmed, how those affirmations informed subsequent behaviors, and so on. I am over time positioned to divest of those ideas that don't serve me well and those ideas that don't serve others.* We argue for the active process of identity deconstructing and reconstructing rooted in humanism and justice.

This includes personal responsibility for behaving, justice-based decision making rooted in the equality of people, engaging interpersonally in ways that honor the varied ways that knowledge and wisdom show up in different bodies, and being personally accountable for self-awareness in interpersonal interactions. These are the makings of the foundation for the identity-conscious community. One that can be accountable for its own health and inclusion, one where the invisible dynamics of inequity and dominance have no place to hide. This is not a process that is accomplished in the space of a training session (although often it is where it starts). This is lifetime work, and in a transformed organization, it becomes a requirement.

Pause and Reflect

What is your intentional practice to deepen your race consciousness?

Why We Can't Problematize Human Beings for Being Human Beings

The overarching theme of this chapter is barriers. Perhaps the biggest barrier to the work of creating our beloved community is simply that we are human. This isn't meant to say that humans don't have the capacity to build a better world. In fact, the core belief that guides this work is the belief in human potential—the potential to learn, to grow, to change. In doing the work of creating the beloved community, where individuals are doing the work of healthy racial identity constructing and transformation of interpersonal dynamics (inter-racially and intra-racially) it is essential that organizations guard against problematizing people for being people. We don't state this to suggest that there be no accountability in this work. The ideas outlined in this book are rooted in accountability, human-centered accountability.

What does human-centered accountability look like? A culture that is built on "call in" rather than "call out" or "cancel culture." As Black women practitioners in this space, it should be clearly stated that we do not take the position that "call out culture" does not have a place. We reserve the right to call out or cancel that which causes trauma, assaults the spirit, intimidates, or is passively resistant. We call in inquiry, courage, bravery, aspirations, and the better expressions of our human selves. We want to invite consideration of elements that cohere people one to another and then ultimately to an organization pursuing a courageous vision of what it can be in the world. What are the bonds necessary to allow extremely challenging conversations and hold space for healing and repair when it is needed? How do people call one another in when they find it an authentic concern for the health and viability of the collective aspiration? These are the questions that colonize the sustaining community that dismantles systems of oppression internally as it seeks to offer supports and services steeped in justice externally.

To that end, we offer that there is both language and dispositional development within such a community that allows its members to problematize practices and not people. In part, this looks like developing ways of being where intents don't overwhelm or nullify actual outcomes. It looks like invitational language to examine different things that are casually stated for deeper meaning and agreement to consider others' perspectives. It is a community where reflection and introspection are normal, a community where conversations that bear multiple visitations receive the attention needed. It is a community that can distinguish the difference between multiple racial perspectives and multiple racist perspectives as the latter are not reified in the community. This is a radical community in that it is relational first, and relational power is the most significant power-based vehicle. The accountability for personal growth, as defined by growth in "cultural competence" is not untethered from other appropriate evidence-based assessments of development. We cannot problema-tize people into growth. We can be critical and decisive in curating the environment that makes space for learning (surfacing, interro-gating, and divesting when needed) and embedding accountability in service of developing a racially conscious community.

When Marginalization Is Practiced in the Community

This section of the chapter will describe common normalized behavioral patterns that can erode community as well as conditions that further intersectional racial equity consciousness develop-ment. *Merriam-Webster* defines *marginalize* this way: "to rele-gate to an unimportant or powerless position within a society or group." This definition helps frame a common organizational inter-personal pattern of behavior. Because all identities are not treated or regarded equally in society, it is typical that marginalization is unconsciously practiced across the organization and within inter-actions between and among staff. Markers of positional power like seniority, credentials, and position are mechanisms that power and disempower. When the CEO or superintendent speaks, their per-spectives are of greater weight and/or importance than those of teachers or students. But what are the consequences of the singular positioning of power of these voices? Very often, those who don't hold formal positions of power are those who hold the very knowl-edge and information that is needed to help the organization serve its intended function.

Those who are purportedly "served" by the organization can see the difference between the talk and the walk with greater clarity than those who formulate the policies that impact them the most. Stu-dents are keenly dialed into the disproportionate treatments across racial lines for similar behaviors, parents have deep insight into a school's communication processes as it allows or inhibits their par-ticipation, and patients have a strong sense of a physician's emotional intelligence by the degree to which they feel seen and heard. The consequences of failing to center the voices and lived experiences of those who are marginalized is to create even wider gaps between what is said versus what is done. Marginalizing voices in a racial con-text most often means minimizing the experiences of people of color, and if the goal is to dismantle structurally inequities, this behavioral pattern must be disrupted.

Journal Prompt

As you consider the preceding text, what are the ways your organization functions in community like this, and in what ways does it not?

Silencing Voices

When organizations problematize conflict and have not normalized the need to develop racial stamina, silencing can be the toxic outcome. First, let's consider problematizing conflict. "Nice" is not an anti-racist strategy, although for many, the presence of "nice" is a smokescreen, that is, an indicator that "those problems don't exist here." Far too often, "nice" is the marker of community health when members of the community have avoided honest discussion of the harm inflicted by racism (and other systems of oppression) to the bodies of those most impacted. Cultures of "nice" can be harmful to people of color and other historically marginalized groups because the "friendliness" on the surface masks the suffering they might experience on a day-to-day basis. When nice is the norm, oppressed people have no space for expression. Moreover, in such environments, racially dominant groups can be totally incredulous to the daily toxicity of the work environment for their non-dominant peers. For this reason, "niceness" must be interrogated for an understanding of its limitations.

Ideas to Sit With

Do you see racialized perspectives treated differently within your organization? What is the pattern you observe?

Some may read this as an undervaluing of cordiality, and nothing could be further from our intention. At the same time, being cordial won't de-center dominance, advance justice, or change the value we give to marginalized perspectives. Conflict is a part of doing racial equity work. More specifically, we need permission to be in conflict with ourselves and our socialization, with our historical patterns of interpersonal engagement, and our organizational practices, policies, and procedures. Unlike conflict that is driven by the desire to dominate, we offer this conflict as the energy for transformation.

Interruptions

Conflating niceness with the presence of justice will not advance racial equity!

The Need to Interrogate the Voices That Surface

When an organization is conflict-averse, those who might offer critical insight can suffer significantly. First, those willing to speak a truth that is disruptive to the dominant narrative can be targeted professionally. Race and gender can greatly impact the consequences we face for questioning the status quo. "Troublemaker," "difficult to work with," not a "team player," "angry": These are the racialized labels that can be affixed to people of color, particularly women of color, when healthy conflict hasn't been normalized. While people who sit in racial dominance can also be penalized for speaking against master narratives of an organization, the consequences are often markedly different than those that are bestowed upon persons of color. For persons of color, speaking our truths can profoundly damage our career trajectories.

If the community aspires to racial equity and anti-racism, the silence breakers should be valued along with the skill associated with this behavior.

Ideas to Sit With

What have you seen as it relates to conflicting voices and career trajectories?

Because This Is Not One Conversation Work

By now, you've probably intuited an important truth: Dismantling institutional racism labor is hard labor. Labor built it; labor will dismantle it. In professional settings, such hard labor is enacted in the form of conversations. How do you come to "see" what is designed for one not to see? This essential question applies to people who live life (and look) like you do, as well as those who don't. Having conversations about race with yourself is important. Having conversations about race with family, church, community organizations, and the like is also important. Maintaining such conversations requires stamina. When White people lack racial stamina, their efforts to engage in anti-racist work are deeply compromised. Yet people of color also need racial stamina. In particular, we must be able to name and heal from racial trauma. We must be able to recognize and divest from harmful internalized Whiteness that reinforces a devaluing of Blackness. The rearrangement of our social relationship depends upon collective participation.

Cultural Invisibility Won't Do

The chapter begins with a quote from Ralph Ellison's book *Invisible Man*, which was published in 1952. Ellison states, "I am invisible, understand, simply because people refuse to see me." While it may be challenging to "see" the culture we live in every day, to see racial hegemony built into our daily norms through organizational policies and other structures, we can advance an anti-racist agenda that interrupts invisibility by engaging with intentionality and curiosity. This intentionality and curiosity can begin with recognition that inequality exists in the organization, even while holding space for all the ways the community may need to come to understand the dimensions of the problem that exists. Again, while this statement may seem audacious, we would suggest that if a community is not working to be expressly anti-racist by engaging in conscious practice and ways of being that de-center Eurocentrism, then it is perpetuating White racial hegemonic ways of being. Hence, action steps around intentionality can include engaging in data reviews to ascertain the racialized trends, holding focus groups with different historically marginalized community members within the organization, and/or interrogating policies using a lens of racial equity to surface any disproportionate impacts that may be occurring. Any of these steps would require leadership and intentionality to make visible how race is shaping access and opportunities within the organization. Curiosity is a posture we recommend because even if one occupies a social location that is marginalized within the institution, there are many intersecting factors that shape experience. For example, while a Black woman may experience a significant amount of isolating and/or avoidance behaviors, a Black transwoman might be experiencing overt harassment like *misgendering* (refusing to use her preferred pronouns). Such curiosity about different lived experiences within the organization will be a driving force in informing our anti-racist policy and practice. Beyond our curiosity, we personally commit to our intra- and inter-racial learning across our organization.

Interruptions

In what ways does your relationship with Blackness and Whiteness need to change?

What Nobody Talks About

Anti-racism cannot be negotiated in spaces where colorblindness abounds. Everyone has responsibility for doing consciousness raising work. Having racialized experiences and having a racial analysis are not synonymous. The team must build accountability for personal and collective engagement for dismantling the invisibility of a marginalizing culture; without accountability, transformation will be threatened.

Your Lived Experience

As you sit with ideas that resonate, given the various dimensions of your identity, answer the following questions:

- What is your role in interrupting invisible aspects of the culture that are anathema to justice and equality?

- In what ways have you started these efforts?

- In what ways are there opportunities that are uniquely yours?

Chapter Reflection

- This chapter examines the role of cultural invisibility and other barriers in creating anti-racist organizations. To what extent have you reflected on the culture of your organization through a lens that exposes how it advantages and disadvantages, includes and excludes? How often is space and time convened for the community to interrogate the culture in this way?

- Among the different ideas advanced in this section, which do you see and experience most often? What impact has it had on the collective from your assessment? Who would you talk with to get a multiple perspective and why?

- How can you work to develop a team of allies within the community to examine and interrogate the organizational mores using an impact over intent model as a means of creating conditions that are unsustaining for inequity?

Part III

Curating Transformation - The Doing Space

Creating Space for Productive Struggle

Joy is the executive administrative assistant for a large non-profit organization. Joy identifies as a Black woman. Following the murder of George Floyd and the social justice uprisings that followed, her executive director, Heather, a White woman, scheduled a staff meeting. At the beginning of the meeting, Heather set the purpose of the meeting as an opportunity to create space for the team to discuss what happened. She then shared how upsetting the whole thing has been for her, how she has lost sleep, how she has been thinking about Joy and her family, and how she has no idea what to do with all her anger. She then asked, "Joy, is there anything you would like to share?" Joy said, "No." Following Joy's very immediate response and after a long period of silence, colleagues commented, "I don't even know what we're talking about." "It is making me extremely uncomfortable to have this conversation at work." "I really want to know what Joy thinks." Heather, who did not anticipate and was unprepared for the responses by the team, ended the meeting. She followed up with Joy and asked why Joy replied "No." In this moment, unbeknownst to Heather, Joy was replaying every racial incident she has ever experienced in the organization. She was quickly able to recount each of them as if they had just occurred. Joy responded by telling her that she did not feel it was best for her to share her feelings because she was not sure people would understand, be able to process, or even appreciate her perspective. In particular, she was disturbed by what people knew and what seemed like a lack of compassion and empathy for what was happening in the world. She noted that George Floyd was not the only person murdered. There was no mention of

Ahmaud Arbery, Breonna Taylor, or the many other lives that had been lost. She offered that as the only Black person on the team and given her place in the organization's hierarchy, she did not want to run the risk of her vulnerability leading to her losing her job. Heather thanked her for being honest. She then informed Joy that she decided that the organization needed to have a committee to help the team with navigating difficult conversations about race so they could become anti-racist. Joy was then charged with being the chair of the new committee, which meant she would research and identify a vendor as well as be the point person for the staff.

Organizations and individuals have little tolerance for the investment required to transform systems and structures that promote equity. For many of us, "investment" is qualified as transactions such as purchasing resources, holding one-off professional development workshops, or hiring consultants with the sole purpose of a quick fix. Heather is a good example of a leader who may be well-intentioned but at the same time could cause harm because she doesn't understand the capacity to appreciate what is needed in the organization. In our context, however, true investment carries a deeper meaning; it requires creating the conditions for people to interrogate and acknowledge not just symptoms but ultimately root causes. This chapter will provide recommendations for how to carefully guide this process and nurture a culture where productive and authentic engagement can occur.

It is often easier to recognize the symptoms of systemic and structural inequities because they are the most obvious. However, a focus solely on symptoms leads to a false sense of resolution. Such a surface-level analysis lacks the specificity to determine the real reason or root cause of the problem. Rarely is there consideration given to the data that should be driving the need to lead anti-racist work. For example, in an educational context, quantitative data may reflect a lower percentage of students of color being admitted to an advanced academics program. On the surface, this could easily appear as straightforward and irrefutable when considering grades, standardized assessments, gifted and talented testing, and teacher recommendations. Conversely, each of those criteria, when closely interrogated, can lead to a deeper understanding of the actual causes for the outcomes. All those criteria, unless sufficiently examined and deliberately controlled, can be riddled with bias. Without the deep reflective work of a root cause analysis centered in racial equity, organizations will be hard-pressed to identify and implement solutions. A thorough analysis of the major contributing factors driving the racial disparity includes quantitative data points, reviews of organizational policies and procedures, and qualitative data that reflect the lived experiences of individuals. This, of course, sounds more simplistic than it is, considering that most organizations grant power to leaders who uphold established organizational norms as well as prescribe transactional ways to engage. Heather, in her role as the executive director, convened a meeting where she thought simply by asking a question or "creating space," the staff would respond and be able to engage in the discussion. Such leadership frequently perpetuates policies and practices that reinforce institutional and structural racism. Typically, such organizations do not take the time to diagnose and understand the culture or assess which aspects of it facilitate change or stand in the way (Heifetz et al., 2009). A failure to do so may result in an inability to recognize how much influence the organizational culture has on acceptable and nonacceptable behavior as well as how each person impacts or is impacted by it.

In the absence of an organizational culture that supports productive and authentic engagement, we cannot be expected to fully lean into, commit to, and sustain discussions about disruption. Once a problem has been identified in an organization, many leadership frameworks suggest that next steps include identifying and implementing an immediate solution. Standard technical "fixes," such as racial equity toolkits, equity look-fors/checklists, and writing strategic plans are unlikely to yield long-term results or eradicate inequitable outcomes. "Organizations and societies alike must resist the impulse to seek immediate relief for the symptoms, and instead focus on the disease" (Livingston, 2020, para. 2). In educational institutions, reaching for the quick fix can prove to be a really dangerous approach, particularly when trying to address systemic and structural inequities. Typical examples include appointing someone in the organization to select a book that everyone needs to read, engaging someone to give a keynote speech, or contracting with a consulting company that purports to help "fix" the organization and the people in it. Such actions are static, yet racial equity is dynamic and requires a more nuanced, deliberate approach. More recently, often in response to the widely publicized racial injustices that surfaced during the summer of 2020, organizations rushed to release statements of solidarity, hired chief equity officers, or launched new departments dedicated to the pursuit of equity and, in many cases, diversity and inclusion. In many cases, these efforts were performative at best because absent interrogating and dismantling internal structures, none of those "acts" will yield transformation and they will be difficult if not impossible to sustain. While these may appear to be more committed responses, they are still guided by the false expectation that after one session or a few hours of an engagement, our "problems" will disappear. In relying on external agents to carry out the labor of equity, we fail to acknowledge the personal commitment of *all* members of the community to explore ways that we may be complicit in the outcomes. Unless we enter this work with clear expectations that we will actively interrogate the roles we play in supporting the status quo, we are more apt to retreat, opt out, and blame the process, rather than taking personal responsibility.

Pause and Reflect

How has your organization created space for you to engage in personal development?

The conscious anti-racist engendering (CARE) framework outlines the personal and interpersonal work that enables us to transition from dysconsciousness (I don't know but I think I do, uncritical racialized knowing) to semi-consciousness (I know I don't know racially, and I am questioning) to consciousness (I know that I know racially). This personal transition creates the conditions to move to institutional and structural transformation. We stand little chance of dismantling deep-rooted institutional and structural inequities without first committing to personal transformation. Central to this transformation is honoring one's humanity. Our greatest opportunity for substantive change begins with the personal and interpersonal work within the community of raising awareness and co-constructing knowledge. Most organizations look at the CARE framework graphic and want to skip to anti-oppression without doing any of the work that most certainly must precede it. Ultimately, leaders must develop an appreciation for how long it takes to shift human behavior.

Figure 6.1   Conscious Anti-Racist Engendering (CARE) Framework

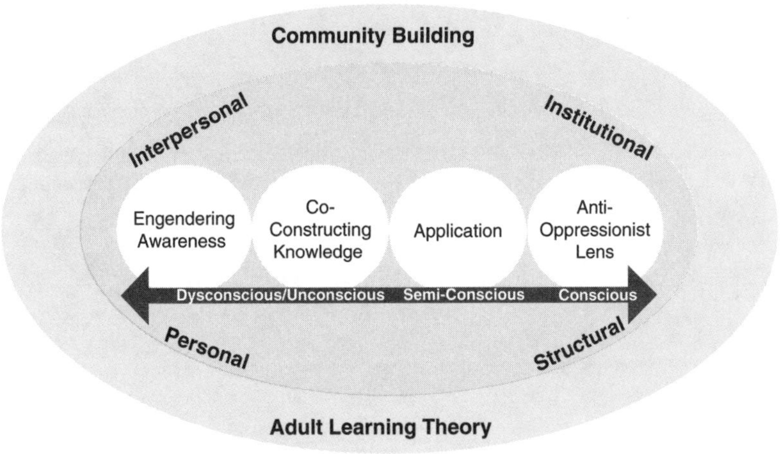

Community Building

Interpersonal   *Institutional*

| Engendering Awareness | Co-Constructing Knowledge | Application | Anti-Oppressionist Lens |

Dysconscious/Unconscious   Semi-Conscious   Conscious

Personal   *Structural*

Adult Learning Theory

However, because of the ways systems function, the urgency of moments like a critical incident in an organization or something external, like another unarmed Black man being killed or a lack of swift justice for the murdering of a Black woman, ignites this need to just *do something,* to create space for people to process, to demonstrate goodness. All without recognition of the potential damage that can be caused by scrambling for a solution, without first engaging in the hard labor of transitioning from dysconsciousness to consciousness. Heather was ill-prepared for the responses by the members of her team. In fact, she was so alarmed by them, she ended the meeting. We must recognize that when the going gets rough (e.g., difficult conversations, conflict within the group), our tendency is to default into White supremacist (or, for some of us, "comfortable") ways of being (Jones & Okun, 2001). Two examples include the following:

Right to Comfort

When someone raises an issue that causes discomfort, the response is to blame the person for raising the issue rather than to look closely at the issue which is actually causing the problem. (Jones & Okun, 2001)

Fear of Open Conflict

And the right to comfort—equating individual acts of unfairness against White people with systemic racism which daily targets people of color. (Jones & Okun, 2001)

Pause and Reflect

What was the last difficult conversation you engaged in professionally?

What conditions must be present for you to be open, honest, and transparent in a difficult conversation?

Do team members trust each other to take risks and be vulnerable?

Whose voices are silenced and whose are privileged?

Productive Struggle

For outcomes to change, organizations must change, and the people in the organization need to change. When we cannot distinguish between symptoms and root causes, we will, at best, mitigate but fail to eradicate inequities. Focusing on symptoms alone restricts the dialogue to the individual rather than structural level.

Achieving racial equity is a dynamic proposition requiring an examination of the multiple levels at which racism operates. One such level, the tip of the iceberg that appears above sea level, represents what is easily recognized and may be mitigated by individuals. The focus on interventions, strategies, and programs may result in short-term successes that do little to change the core, the base, and the fundamental inequities that permeate the organization. The result is that the inequities are masked and less detectable, but they still exist. The larger part of the iceberg—the piece that sits below the water—represents the deep structure or root cause and is only mitigated when there is organizational awareness, knowledge, and decision making rooted in anti-racism. Otherwise, the persistent, stubborn, and hard to eliminate structures will persist and exacerbate.

Organizations often publicly espouse their commitment to external practice without first investing in building internal capacity. Building interpersonal (racial) capacity at the "micro" level is an essential component and a prerequisite to transforming systems. Structural racism is persistent, pernicious, and complex. We will not succeed in unseating it without taking the time to hone our understanding of the macro forces that perpetuate it (the below sea-level part of the iceberg), including our large-scale systems, institutions, social forces, and ideologies (Powell, 2008).

The journey to anti-racism requires individual and organizational capacity building. The CARE framework begins with engendering awareness in a culture where risk, transparency, trust, and vulnerability are encouraged, honored, valued, and welcomed. By now, it should be clear that creating such conditions takes time and investment. To achieve this at all levels of the organization can cause considerable stress for employees, especially those of color who are often asked to carry the burden of anti-racist efforts. Fong-Olivares (2018) writes, "If not tactfully managed, issues of intersectionality, power dynamics, personal and work-related boundaries, and unconscious biases can become barriers that stand in the way of progress" (para. 2).

Engaging in anti-racism work forces us to come to terms with uncomfortable truths. Our nation has had a dreadful history of dehumanization and an insidious relationship with devaluing perspectives that run contrary to the dominant narrative of White supremacy. Most of our organizations are grounded in this narrative, in that they do not center anti-racism as a core value. In such settings, we may be called upon to engage in racialized conversations that begin without any shared understanding, language, and skill to engage. Such conversations easily lead to anxiety, stress, and even trauma for participants, especially people of color. When this happens, the default response is to decrease the tension, stop the conversation, and sometimes step aside from the work. It's the reason the staff couldn't and wouldn't engage in the discussion during the meeting with Heather. Anti-racism requires leaning into a productive struggle. A productive struggle is one that requires organizations to interrogate power, honor perspectives, examine self, anticipate conflict, and learn (unlearn) history (IHEAL).

Interruptions

Systems and structures are made up of people. Therefore, systems don't change until the people do.

Interrogate Power

Those who have authority can weaponize their power, albeit unintentionally. In these aspirational moments, those who have the least power in the organization are those who are often asked to lead the work and shepherd the organization through this period of learning, reconciliation, and healing. For example, the only person of color on a team is asked to lead equity work, the only board member of color is asked to lead the equity subcommittee, a new higher education faculty member is told they must join the senate subcommittee on inclusion. If it is true, as Collins (2012) asserts, that power relationships shape who is believed and who is disbelieved, those in powerful positions of leadership have a unique responsibility to engage directly in productive struggle themselves; otherwise, they risk harming those who are already the most vulnerable in the organization.

Honor Perspectives

Singleton (2015) writes, "My intention is not that we validate another's story but rather we validate that each of us has a story, and more than likely, our stories will be somewhat different" (p. 119). Among many of the reasons these conversations are difficult is our tendency as humans to want to be right rather than the desire to communicate. It is often easy and even acceptable to dismiss someone's narrative when there is disagreement or, quite frankly, lack of understanding. Different perspectives can cause considerable dissonance because they often conflict with our own beliefs and worldviews.

Examine Self

James Baldwin stated that history is something "we carry within us [and] are unconsciously controlled by." A journey to building racial consciousness calls upon us to evaluate what race has meant in one's life and an examination of how it is lived every day. We can devour history books and build our theoretical knowledge, but, above all, we need to make this exploration one that is personal. In particular, we need to come to terms with our own role in perpetuating systems of oppression.

Anticipate Conflict

Anticipating conflict requires full recognition of how individuals wrestle with and reconcile the need to be comfortable. When conversations about *-isms* are centered in a deep and meaningful way, conflict is bound to be present. In fact, it is not a question of *if* there will be conflict because there will be. In preparing for this inevitable result, we need to carefully consider which voices will be privileged and which will be problematized. Often, when the conflict happens, those with the least amount of power in the organization are hyper visible and are therefore silenced. When creating the conditions in a way that gives full recognition to this as a phenomenon, attention must be given to how easy it is to prioritize a privileged person's comfort over another's humanity.

Learn (Unlearn) History

We cannot fully engage in the personal and interpersonal development process without first recognizing that we may not understand the historical context of race. Our knowledge building should examine the impact of race on ourselves and on our country, as well as how race plays out in our local context. For educational institutions, non-profits, and other organizations, this includes the local jurisdiction, neighborhoods, political landscape, and so on. In the words of James Baldwin, "What one begs the American people to do, for all our sakes, is simply to accept our history."

There is a relationship between and among individuals, positions they hold, and the organizations in which they work. This interdependent relationship demands a critical analysis and ability to anticipate how individuals of different racial groups engage in productive struggle and respond to discomfort. Organizations that fully lean into the productive struggle do so in full recognition that the skills of "understanding history, interrogating personal biases, building empathy and respect for others, and getting comfortable with vulnerability . . . require training and ongoing practice" (Hecht, 2020, para. 11).

What Nobody Talks About

You are either perpetuating or interrupting. There is no middle ground. Interruption takes deliberate action and intent. Therefore, if you are unable to name how you are interrupting, you are perpetuating.

Your Lived Experience

Your willingness to lean into who you are and how you have made meaning in the world matter if ultimately what you want is to be different.

- It is not enough to simply desire to be different. How will you commit to shedding all that you think you know and understand about the world?

- The new learning you will undoubtedly experience does not mean everything you learned is problematic. What will it require for you to be open to the possibility that some of what you know, or what you think you know, requires interrogation?

Chapter Reflection

- What do you think colleagues of different racial groups will need in order to engage? How do you know?

- Who is charged with leading the organization's anti-racist efforts? How have they been authorized to lead the work? How has this been communicated to the rest of the organization?

- What strategy will be used when people struggle and experience dissonance with new learning?

- Who is accountable for desired outcomes, and what does that accountability include?

Application of Equity Lens for System Change   7

> *Not everything that is faced can be changed, but nothing can be changed until it is faced.*
>
> James Baldwin

Dr. Alise Fale is a system leader who provides support and coaching for school leaders at all levels. During the health pandemic, several concerns were raised regarding how students and families were experiencing instruction in the virtual world. The school district had sent out many surveys to families and staff leading up to the start of the school year to gain a better understanding of what supports were needed to ensure access to effective instruction. Outside of the growing concerns that still lingered regarding health and health care access, it became clear that virtual learning widened longstanding imbalances of access and opportunity to learn among different student populations. After having several district-level meetings and hearing from multiple stakeholders, Dr. Fale began to ruminate on how this pandemic was truly impacting students' academic attainment. Aside from broadband connectivity disparities, the virtual learning environment limited access to differentiated and individualized instruction—essential supports that many students needed in order to learn. She knew her activism had to employ out-of-the-box thinking as well as be deliberate in not perpetuating institutionalized practices that further marginalize students. There were indeed challenges with digital learning. There had to be a way she could advocate; at that moment, an idea came to her. The next day, she met with her high school building leaders and posed the following question: "What are your thoughts regarding eliminating final exams?" The immediate responses were "We cannot do this. How will we assess their learning? This is not the direction at the collegiate level." Dr. Fale could not believe the overwhelming counter response and knew that she had to work on uncovering the base of their knowledge to reframe what's necessary in order to be responsive to students in this moment of crisis.

Pause and Reflect

Think of a time when you foresaw the need for out-of-the-box thinking that disrupted the normal way of doing. What was the idea? What was the response? What was the outcome?

Dr. Fale's dilemma is all too common. Leaders across multiple organizations and levels find themselves trying to disrupt systems of oppression that marginalize specific groups of people and are met with resistance. Dr. Fale responded to the moment, allowing lived experiences to create a new normal and knowing that change, though difficult, was necessary. She layered her concerns with what was happening nationally. Across the country, Black bodies disproportionately became ill and perished due to the COVID-19 pandemic while simultaneously, Black men and women were losing their lives at the hands of police officers from multiple states. In response to the two pandemics—health crisis and racial inequity—Dr. Fale applied an equity lens to her own context and devised a way to ensure that students were not further marginalized. How could it be that school leaders didn't see this as beneficial? In the midst of such unprecedented crises, how could they fail to recognize that an adaptive response was urgently needed?

Think back to James Baldwin's statement about history in the previous chapter. In what ways has our understanding of history influenced our ways of being and knowing as well as how we make decisions? Regardless of our skin color, gender, and other social identifiers, if our beliefs and values are constructed around an assumption of Whiteness as a norm, our actions will be in alignment. Because our educational system was formed around Eurocentric values, practices, and processes, many of us take for granted the manner in which we have internalized Whiteness. This chapter will explore the process of de-centering Whiteness and centering the work of building anti-racist spaces. In particular, we explore how to leverage the conscious anti-racist engendering (CARE) framework in the interest of working collaboratively to dismantle systems of oppression that have historically marginalized groups of students, specifically those of color.

We will identify specific moves that can be used by system leaders to promote close examination of systemic structures, processes, and practices that were formed around Eurocentric values that privileged the needs of those of the dominant culture. This will require an examination of qualitative and quantitative data and a shift from using transactional processes alone as these will not impact outcomes. Like Dr. Fale's solution, the leadership that is called for to interrupt predictable outcomes based on race must be transformational and adaptive.

Moving Past Productive Struggle

We want to, again, underscore the importance of the concept of productive struggle mentioned in the previous chapter. In the framework of teaching and learning, Hammond (2015) defines productive struggle as "when the learner has developed the necessary strategies for working through something difficult" (p. 156). In the context of racial equity work, such "struggle" can come in the form of the dissonance we experience when we are exposed to multiple perspectives that are different from our own. Without such productive struggle, our trajectory toward becoming anti-racist on the individual and organizational levels will be prolonged and/or not achieved. The CARE framework commits that because of this process, community is essential for the journey of becoming anti-racist. The application of an equity lens means that there is a "process for analyzing or diagnosing the impact of the design and implementation of policies on under-served and marginalized individuals and groups, and to identify and potentially eliminate barriers" (University of Minnesota, para. 3). When we commit to anti-racist policies and practices, we commit to understanding the historical connections to our present-day practices and how they have remained steeped in Whiteness.

Let's consider the critical landmark cases mentioned in Chapter 1 and make some connections as we travel back in time. The 1896

Plessy v. Ferguson decision allowed for the federal government to officially recognize segregation as legal when the U.S. Supreme Court ruled that Louisiana had the right to require "separate but equal" facilities. Fast forward some 58 years later to *Brown v. Board of Education of Topeka* (1954) in which the Supreme Court abolished segregated schools citing them as "inherently unequal," yet schools, especially in the North, were still segregated. Then in 1957, the nation saw the monumental coverage of the Little Rock Nine as the governor of Arkansas sent the National Guard to physically prevent nine Black students from enrolling in all-White Central High School, following the federal court order to integrate Arkansas public schools. Let's move to the 1974 case, *Milliken v. Bradley,* when the Supreme Court ruled that schools may not be desegregated—a decision that, once again, effectively segregated students of color from White people. Despite all the efforts around desegregation, there are still states with cases in education fighting to desegregate in the 21st century. One example is the 2011 case of *Cowan and United States v. Bolivar County Board of Education No. 4.* We know that history rhymes; because patterns repeat themselves by failing to apply an equity lens to education policies and practices, we are likely to encounter new manifestations of systemic oppression that further marginalizes people of color. As we've emphasized, unseating deep-rooted systems of oppression that have endured for centuries will not be accomplished with quick-fix solutions, but when we are willing to engage in productive struggle, we are more likely to effect lasting change.

Ideas to Sit With

Where is White dominance (historical reference) present in your current work? What actions are you being called to do?

Modern-Day Schooling

As we understand the evolution of education and its impact on modern-day schooling, we cannot ignore the presence of dominant culture as an influencer. It is this dominant culture that situates outcomes for all students, even the undesired outcomes. Understand that racial dominant thinking gives racially dominant advantages. For example, the adoption of Common Core State Standards, now

College and Career Readiness Standards, created by the Council of Chief State School Officers (CCSSO) and supported by the Obama administration, were never intended to be a "national curriculum." The only requirement was that states have "challenging state academic standards" for those states that opted in. That requirement was broadly interpreted, and not all states opted in. This adoption, like decades of school reform, had an over-reliance on standardized testing as a measure of potential and/or growth, which is a great flaw. The origins of such tests are closely aligned to the Eugenics movement in the United States with a primary purpose to sort students—much in the manner of Thomas Jefferson's vision of education for the elite.

These assessments are still doing exactly what they intended to do. Not only are such tests culturally biased, but the absurd idea that a child's future can rest on a single data point was rarely called into question during the No Child Left Behind (NCLB) era. Moreover, this mania to quantify every aspect of human experience is, in itself, grounded in White supremacist thinking. It's true that the Elementary and Secondary Education Act (ESEA), throughout its various iterations, was intended to advance equity, but the standards and tests that formed the core of these "reforms" were examples of technical solutions applied to adaptive challenges.

One addition to this reauthorization was the intentional focus on advancing equity by requiring that all students be educated to be successful for college and or career paths. If you understand how dominant culture works, you will know that this system, even with a national commitment to ensuring equal opportunity for all students, with an intended frame on success within college and/or career, would fail students who are not of the dominant culture.

The pervasive and deliberate lack of acknowledgment of misalignment of standardized assessment data demonstrates why it is important to understand how systems designed using Eurocentric values are a detriment to students who are of color and not culturally connected to these same values by which our educational system is grounded. The results of these assessments appear to show that students are failing, but the test, given its design, is biased and creates a false dichotomy. Should this assessment be used to drive what students get, or is it a false predictor of what students are destined for? The answer to that question is a resounding NO! A number of U.S. presidents and secretaries of education have, over many years, identified education as the great civil rights issue of our time (Au, 2019). Whether we are discussing the NAEP, SAT, ACT, or any other standardized assessments, we recognize that there is an achievement gap that is presently based on race. These assessments are not achieving educational equity and do not serve students of color (Au, 2019). The results of standardized tests are predictable by race as these assessments are not race neutral.

Part of interrogating systemic racism in our schools is acknowledging the impact of standardized assessments on outcomes for students of color. Begin by asking yourself, what exactly are we measuring, and why is it important? We are failing students of color because we are centering Whiteness by relying on a system that was never intended to promote success for them. Although it is common knowledge that Black students, students of color, and those who are economically disadvantaged typically score lower on standardized assessments in comparison to their White peers, the deep-seated reasons for such outcomes often remain hidden. The reasons become clear only when we apply an equity lens in the service of interrupting these predictable patterns; equity of voice through lived experiences must prevail.

The CARE framework underscores the importance or personal and organizational introspection. Education agencies, organizations, and leaders share the need for taking an introspective stance—no less than a close examination of how we got to this point, what we need to interrupt, and how to reimagine moving forward in authentic relationship genuinely promoting and guaranteeing success for Black students.

The 2002 reauthorization of the ESEA (also known as the No Child Left Behind Act [NCLB]) introduced stricter accountability provisions ("consequences") for schools that continually showed achievement disparities between racial groups (again, based on the results of high-stakes test scores). The latest iteration of ESEA (the Every Student Succeeds Act [ESSA]) shifted regulatory (accountability) responsibilities to state and local education agencies. Over this period of nearly two decades, school leaders grappled with the daunting task of leading these educational institutions with the goal of producing students who are college and career ready.

Despite significant investments in fiscal and human capital to achieve such outcomes, most efforts have failed. When transactional, technical solutions (framed in the guise of "school reform") fail, leaders typically don't have the supports that lead to transformative actions. Again, ask yourself the question, *What are we measuring and why?* In the absence of meaningful metrics that place Black students at the core, history will continue to rhyme. This leads us to the next critical question: If not "the way it's always been done," then what are the data we need to analyze?

Transformative Processes Call for an Analysis of All Data

Educational leaders across multiple agencies have been empowered to lead the major work of ensuring all students are college and career ready beyond the preK–12 experience. These leaders must be deliberate in their actions. It is only through the intentional disruption of these systems that we can ensure educational equity that effectively attends to the needs of students who are historically marginalized. Our goal is to ensure outcomes are no longer predictable based on race. Reflective and action-oriented leaders understand the role they have in ensuring focus on students as individuals. An equity-focused leader does not just focus on numbers. We have to move beyond limiting ourselves analyzing quantitative data such as standardized test results and concede that improving instruction can only be achieved through both quantitative *and* qualitative analysis.

When we apply qualitative and quantitative data-driven decision making to planning content, grouping students, and selecting instructional strategies, resources, and interventions, we have to understand what these data signify and the relative importance of our data points. Summative assessment data, alone, cannot be the driver for making decisions that impact students' success. In the two decades following the passage of NCLB, federal legislation that required state and local educational agencies (SEAs and LEAs) to disaggregate achievement data (based on a single data point, state assessments) indicates that disparities haven't narrowed. This fact alone provides evidence of the failings of the "logic model" that we have applied to school reform. It is obvious that inequities will persist. In this moment, with community established and continuing to grow cohesive, the instructional leader is prepared to step back in order to elevate the multiple perspectives of the leadership team. This will allow for the creation of norms that will drive the work of ensuring successful and positive student outcomes because marginalized students are centered for decision making due to the implementation of equity-based leadership actions. Let's consider an educational leader's experience.

> *Mr. Leak, a building leader moving through his equity journey, is frustrated with the school system's yearly published chart of school rankings based on performance of the state assessment. His school has appeared in the middle area for the past two years and is making slow improvements. He cannot understand why scores are not improving exponentially as he and his staff have committed to using data when making instructional decisions. He has routine leadership meetings, instructional leadership teams, and collaborative teaming to discuss student data and action steps for teachers. When the team observes classes, they see small group instruction and, for the most part, content aligned to the standards.*

Interruptions

Considering this leader's journey, what are the transformational components that must be present?

The preceding scenario describes all the transitional items that are perceived as grounded in data, the quantitative data, but what about the missing data, that which is qualitative? The personal, informative experience of school and instruction of students is found when exploring the qualitative impact while seeking to understand the numbers, or the reason(s) behind the numbers. In the current educational landscape, district and building leaders employ an analysis process for quantitative data that explores the aggregate and on occasion will disaggregate by race, gender, and instructional setting but hardly ever explore the intersection of qualitative and quantitative data. In the intersection, the stories behind the numbers—the lived experiences of students and their families—are made visible. The effectiveness of the leadership team is rooted in creating community that honors individual and collective knowledge as the origin of the team's process. In such community, we openly speak of our own experiences, our work influences, and name how and why system-centered institutionalized practices harm students of color. Through these multiple experiences new norms emerge, and we transition from gap conversations that loosely get to the root cause or the "why" of the data to productive conversations regarding the "who, what, why, and how" that provide the narrative to shape adult actions. The critical steps to analyzing qualitative and quantitative data are essential to the functioning of an equity-infused leadership team. The steps outlined in Figure 7.1 are practice indicators leading considerations for instructional leadership teams to explore when analyzing data and becoming transformational.

Figure 7.1   Qualitative and Quantitative Data for Analysis

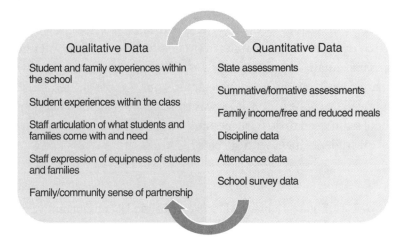

As teams work together within community on co-constructing knowledge that will create an environment that centers students of color and their families, they evolve their level of consciousness and begin to apply the necessary lens to effectively make decisions. These decisions are not arbitrary. They are deliberate and entrenched in the data points identified in Figure 7.1. As in the root cause analysis process, one interrogates the "why" until one understands what is to be interrupted so that transformation ensues. When we limit ourselves to analyzing quantitative data, we fail to get a full picture, including the historical context that helps us to understand—for example, *why* students of color and those who are economically disadvantaged are over-represented in special education. If we want to eliminate predictable outcomes based on race, we have to center on race and equity by applying a racial equity lens in decision making.

When operating within the CARE framework, team members work continuously for years to consciously apply such a lens to all decisions that influence outcomes for historically marginalized populations. These decisions are carried out after going through the challenging process of analyzing *all* relevant data that will inform practices for educators. When people within community reach the highest level of racial consciousness, the marginalized students who have been negatively impacted by these historically oppressive systems are centered. The best interest of those who are often left out is elevated. The once forgotten become the sages on the stage. And we no longer have to endure a system riddled with institutionalized racist practices as we leverage our power to dismantle these practices one action at a time. When we reach this stage, all aspects of education will be prioritized and positively impacted.

Figure 7.2 describes key areas that need to be intentionally examined by decision-making adults in the context of schooling as it interrupts marginalized practices. By centering these students, the power dynamic shifts as the actionable adult steps are predicated on student needs. So, one may ask, how is this accomplished? What does a school team need to do to successfully transform an environment so that all students meet with success?

Figure 7.2   Equity-Centered Decision Making Using Qualitative and Quantitative Data

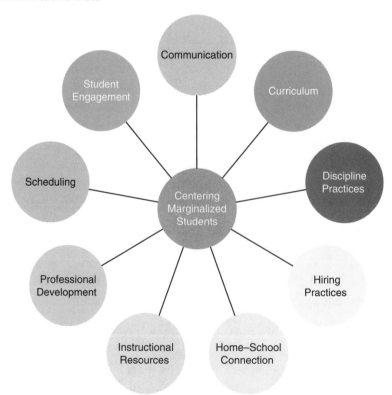

When we center marginalized students, we have to apply a lens that centers race while attending to other aspects of students' identities as a means of interrogating how the system functions with regard to multiple areas. This same intersection used for applying a racial equity lens must be understood for educational components because they do not act in silos; we have to appreciate how our hiring practices have implications for scheduling and discipline practices. The same holds true for scheduling, discipline practices, and student engagement. If we consider the areas of focus within Figure 7.2 and apply an intersectional racial equity lens to our decision making, the examples to follow will demonstrate what transformation looks like in that area so that it can yield the intended outcomes for marginalized students.

- **Communication:** Organizations create structures in which communication is provided in multiple languages for ease and readability for staff, students, families, and communities. Additionally, there are resources provided that demonstrate open, two-way dialogue that honors all stakeholders and invites multiple perspectives to inform how communication is created based on feedback.

- **Curriculum:** Curriculum is not school specific but instead adopted by school districts, so using appropriate resources, trainings, and parent workshops would be added to help create an environment where curriculum is augmented to meet the needs of students while offering supplemental resources to ensure exposure to grade-level standards-aligned instruction. The expectation would be for teachers to build their capacity of the materials through professional learning while seeking to understand how students are using relationship-building strategies as well as data to drive planning and implementation of instruction.

- **Discipline Practices:** The removal of "non-negotiables" and strict adherence to the code of conduct will be replaced with individualized approaches to understanding each case as a separate and exclusive situation that honors the students and members experiencing the event when students demonstrate behaviors not aligned to written disciplinary policies and procedures. School staff will adopt positive behavior interventions and supports and commit to the appropriate infusion of clinical supports as well as regular training for school-based staff around cultural understanding, age-appropriate behaviors, and analyzing discipline data to align adult actions and supports to ensuring school communities are safe, supportive, and nurturing educational environments. As school leaders make the adjustments to the handling of disciplinary concerns based on student actions, they can then merge these efforts as part of a collaborative function with district office teams. These efforts can be used to inform the co-construction of new policies and procedures governing how school systems handle discipline.

- **Hiring Practices:** There is a consideration of what each place needs based on what support or productivity is necessary. Educator placement will be contingent upon student need (based on educational setting), and processes will reflect structures that no longer eliminate people of color at the hiring table. Therefore, hiring panels are diversified to include considerations of race, gender, ethnicity, educational level, and other factors, as well as representation from all stakeholder groups elevating parental input. The advancement of candidates exhibiting various racial, gender, and ethnic backgrounds will allow for the diversification of environments because of the increased availability of candidates.

- **Home–School Connection:** There will be use of communication that is translated based on the languages spoken within the community. The input of families will be sought using multiple forums to maximize participation, and outreach will occur as part of the climate and culture of the building. Stakeholder meetings will occur at different times throughout the day as well as through technology, in person or by phone to capture working families and those with other obligations. There will be proper use of clinical staff to provide access to wrap-around services and resources based on need.

- **Instructional Resources:** Because curriculum is not school specific in most cases, there will need to be instructional resources that are supplemental to the curriculum. These resources will aid students in accessing grade-level, standards-aligned content by having technology-based enhancements. These resources will cater to various learning modalities and have an at-home connection, where applicable. There will be culturally relevant components that enhance the teaching and learning for students.

- **Professional Development:** The learning for staff will be scaffolded based on capacity of the adult learner while considering those who are receiving instruction and their needs. There will be culturally relevant content infused in this tiered, ongoing job and embedded opportunities that provide transferrable information for staff to use within the learning environment.

- **Scheduling:** Students' academic and social needs are centered such that scheduling is reflective of the timing of mod classes necessary to facilitate the instructional model time frame based on best practices for all content areas. There is flexibility with content classes that allow for rotation to avoid students' possibly missing instruction in a specific area daily. There is the opportunity for access to grade-level instruction with room for mediation and response to intervention.

- **Student Engagement:** Instructional environments will be places where adults act as facilitators of learning by endorsing student-shared ownership in decision making around environmental and academic mores. Students will be responsible to each other by holding space for engaging in academic discourse and using co-constructed systems to interface with peers around project-based learning that is relevant to their lived experiences and culturally connected. There is equity in voice-elevated and embedded systems of management that support the peer-to-peer coaching and feedback process to build on each other's understanding. The teacher's responsibility within this environment is to

Pause and Reflect

In the concept of transformative leadership, the examples as outlined may seem intuitive. However, what is the leader's role in ensuring adult accountability for guaranteeing communities of belonging and helping individuals understand their racialized selves within these spaces?

uplift and normalize multiple perspectives so that diverse needs are met and students' brilliance can flourish.

The solution is not as complex as one might imagine. It is only when our actions are a product of our personal and communal work that calls upon us to be introspective about beliefs, bias, teaching, and experiences, that the potential for transformation can be fully realized.

Interruptions

Is there a recognition of the role I, as an individual, play in perpetuating or interrupting racist practices that oppress those who are marginalized?

Each of us enter into the community as an imperfect individual, each with our own blemishes, each bearing our own implicit biases and experiences that shape our actions and expectations. Our task is to plan, implement, and drive practices that are informed by anti-racist ways of being to guarantee transformation. As the team collaborates and creates new systems and structures, they will be able to dismantle former systems that perseverated institutionalized racist practices. The goal is to reimagine a process that is adaptive and not technical, transformative and not transactional, and suffused in re-humanization.

Ultimately, system leaders, of all racial groups, need to make decisions that are contrary to our normal way of being. We cannot expect to be anti-racist in a racist system, especially when people are unable to see beyond a lens of Whiteness. As we become transformative in our thinking, ways of being, practices, and considerations, we have to know that race and racism matter when we are attempting to disrupt, dismantle, and interrupt racist systems and institutions. We acknowledge that we have all made an investment in White supremacy to become leaders within organizations built on Eurocentric values and beliefs. However, transformation means leaders are showing up in their full power, being courageous and preparing the next generation for greatness.

What Nobody Talks About

When being a transformational equity leader, the body you sit in will determine the narrative being propelled; allies in this work will be critical. Race and racism matter when you are disrupting a system. Leaders of color, like all other leaders, have invested in White supremacy. Black leaders have to mobilize when they take a seat at the table to promote change.

Your Lived Experience

Being transformative as an equity leader means that you acknowledge how historically racist systems have oppressed people of color and others who are marginalized.

- How does the historical education context that has normed your present educational experience different from the qualitative and quantitative areas examined in this chapter? How does this new learning move you to action?

- How do you use adaptive leadership skills to advance wisdom from your community?

- What have you learned about the ways your actions must change to center students of color and those being marginalized and to disrupt systems and predictable educational outcomes based on race?

Chapter Reflection

- How do you usher people into a state of consciousness that acknowledges that numbers (quantitative) do not mean more than lived experiences (qualitative)?

- How do you as an equity leader balance knowledge from a book with that of knowledge from the community?

- If the nature of knowing is formed through White supremacy, what are your leadership steps to create new legacies?

Building to Transformation Through Collective Application

8

Although True Elementary School has 25 teachers, Ms. Jackson and Mrs. Lewis are the only Black teachers on the staff. Ms. Jackson is a teacher at Michael's school. (You may remember Michael and Jonathan, our favorite kindergartners from our opening chapter.) Ms. Jackson has a love of teaching. She is devoted to her profession and has dreamed of making a difference for students, especially students of color. Raised on a firm belief that education is the equalizer, Ms. Jackson provides her best teaching each day for her students. She relates to their struggle—being a Black female in a society that does not honor Black skin. When she was a student, her teachers often viewed her as "academically disposable," despite her best efforts to demonstrate the values aligned with the dominant cultural expectations of being a "good" student. Upon introspection and reflection, Ms. Jackson realized the commonalities between her personal education story and the current story of the Black students at True Elementary School. As a student, Ms. Jackson was marginalized by teachers who did not have high expectations for her, and she was labeled based on the same attributes she shared with her current students. Ms. Jackson persevered through institutionalized racism and sexism to achieve her goals of teaching students of color. Dismantling the cycle was the only option to yield different outcomes for students of color. Ms. Jackson believes in the ability of her students to learn and achieve at high levels. The students' futures made her want to work harder for them. "Not on my watch" is the mantra that Ms. Jackson lives by. Ms. Jackson acknowledges and volunteers to be a voice advocating for students of color. She does not view it as a responsibility but instead sees it as her call to action. Speaking to issues of race and questioning practices in meetings have created an uncomfortable dynamic between Ms. Jackson and other teachers. Although Ms. Jackson is known for her positive interactions and relationships with all stakeholders, staff members often ostracize her and won't engage with her. During meetings, leaders do not hear her voice. Staff members cut her off when she is speaking, dismiss her ideas or suggestions, and don't invite her to social events.

Often these hurtful actions are subtle. For example, staff members will indicate she has a great idea but then fail to openly support the idea when others are present. She is praised for being able to "work" with the Black and Brown parents. Fellow teachers only ask her questions related to the management of students and do not engage her in conversations related to instructional practices. An environment that was once welcoming has become toxic to Ms. Jackson. Ms. Jackson feels alone in her pursuit of equity for Black students in her building and is considering transferring to another school. In her experiences, she feels alone, and she questions if they are on the same team.

Pause and Reflect

What are the indicators causing the toxic environment? How does racial identity development speak to these issues?

What does the cultural pattern suggest?

As the racial equity leader, how can you disrupt the indicators causing the toxic environment?

Black people *can* and *do* experience racism in all aspects of life. Ms. Jackson's experience is common, especially for a Black teacher working to change the trajectory for students of color, especially when working to interrupt and transform the relationships among power, race, and racism. Educators frequently engage in conversations about any number of education topics with minimal discomfort. However, what may not be apparent is that such "normal" conversations are also framed by a racialized lens—the dominant lens of Whiteness. When we begin to racialize topics outside of the Whiteness lens, emotions and discomfort frequently surface (Brewley-Kennedy, 2005). Battey and Leyva (2016) connect such levels of discomfort to DiAngelo's (2011) work on *White Fragility,* characterized by "silence, fear guilt, or avoiding discussions about race altogether, which serves to reproduce the status quo of white supremacy" (p. 53). In Ms. Jackson's situation, the discomfort of the adults has taken priority over the outcomes for students of color.

The resulting behaviors of avoidance, dismissal, and the overall isolation of Ms. Jackson and all she represents will ultimately harm her students if she is driven to transfer to another school. Ms. Jackson's situation is not unique, as demonstrated by a body of research that argues that Black female teachers on predominately White faculties often experience unfair, unrealistic expectations (Milner, 2020). The same researcher contends that Black female teachers are expected to be team players and agree with the White majority even when they disagree (Milner, 2020).

Interruptions

Why is it necessary to interrupt the norming and continuation of practices that are counter to advancing the community toward transformative practices?

What are the potential consequences of not interrupting?

In continuing to move the collective to higher levels of consciousness, we must be willing to commit to the action of interrupting racist practices and structures that continue to benefit some at the expense of others. Although racial equity leaders are expected to provide the necessary guidance to unseat systems of oppression, interruption is a collective process that requires active participation from the entire collective (community). Ms. Jackson's experience is an example of a racialized dynamic within the collective group.

This chapter will examine the importance of co-constructing conditions using an anti-oppression lens to engage in transformative practices that interrupt predictable patterns for students of color. The community will need language and process to pose challenges within the collective, and, when warranted, to push back when individual members of the collective cannot move beyond the Eurocentric lens. This is especially important because (as previously indicated) people arrive along their equity journey with different levels of consciousness and capacity. However, no matter the level of consciousness, the collective is still steeped in the norms of Whiteness. This chapter will provide suggestions and strategies to move staff from discomfort to healthy discussion while creating a supportive environment for accountability toward racially equitable results.

Supportive Environment: An Understanding, a Feeling, and an Experience

Ms. Jackson's situation is a vivid example of some of the nuances involved in racialized situations. As a racial equity leader, an approach that names and unpacks those nuances is needed to co-construct a supportive environment to address the needs of the collective as they build their racial equity. The concept of support for a racial equity leader is demonstrated in action. Words without a supporting act do not yield a feeling of support. Building the collective and engaging all voices in a supportive environment while respecting their humanity and individuality is a catalyst to transformative action.

Figure 8.1   Conscious Anti-Racist Engendering (CARE) Framework

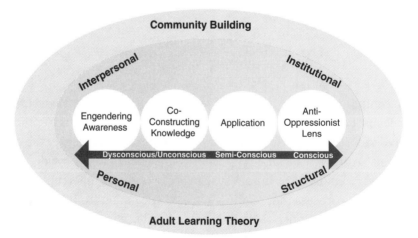

Recall that the conscious anti-racist engendering (CARE) framework identifies the capacity needs of the individual as well as the collective

while moving from dysconsciousness to consciousness to impact outcomes for students of color. Again, let's return to Ms. Jackson's dilemma as an example. In this situation, Ms. Jackson is expected to "play nice," that is, adhere to the norms of Whiteness. However, if this dynamic is not dismantled, there will be no change for the students or Ms. Jackson. The collective is charged with co-constructing conditions to de-center the dominant narrative and apply those conditions with the explicit intention of ensuring practice from an anti-oppressive lens. To sharpen your understanding of what this looks like, we use the acronym SAUCE (support, accountable, uproot, co-construct, elevate) to describe specific conditions that elevate and enhance transformative efforts for students of color (adapted from Dixon et al., 2019). More information and examples of the application associated with SAUCE will follow in the chapter.

An example of supporting agency is encouraging educators to process topics and situations with a racialized lens. We work to facilitate such processing and enable educators to be "critical friends" with one another. In this way, we build the capacity for autonomy or for educators to act with levels of consciousness independently. We extend this to mean one who provides data to be examined through a racialized lens and offers critique as a professional friend. While advocating for success, a critical friend understands the context of the work and the outcomes of the person or group (Costa & Kallick, 1993).

As a racial equity leader, you provide support to foster independence—similar to a teacher operating in a student's zone of proximal development. The goal is to empower the staff to claim their agency in the interest of designing a learning environment where Black students are not invisible. Through engaging in conversations about race, the work becomes a shared experience, and the engagement builds community.

Accountable and Free From Alienation

During a conversation with Ms. Jackson, she shared,

> Ms. Tallador and I worked on an attendance project together. Ms. Tallador, at the time, had a really hectic schedule, and I designed and completed the project without much help from her. The team loved the project. The team assumed Ms. Tallador did all the work. They showered her with

compliments. Not once did Ms. Tallador correct them and acknowledge my work. And I just sat there waiting for her to acknowledge my work. My ideas are not valued when people know they are my ideas. When I do share an idea, it is dismissed. When someone else says the same idea, it is the best idea ever. Full steam ahead for implementation on my idea but only through someone else. So, help me understand, if my idea is valued, then why does it lose value when it comes from me?

None of us wants to work in an environment that is inhospitable, antipathetic, and polarizing. Alienation does not always present in an overt manner, as evidenced by the experience of Ms. Jackson when others appropriated or failed to acknowledge her for her ideas. Accountability includes a commitment to build a space in which no one is isolated from the collective and our contributions are valued.

Uprooting Racial Microaggressions

As the racial equity leader, there must be an awareness and dedication to identifying and uprooting racial microaggressions occurring in the environment, "Racial microaggressions are . . . daily verbal, behavioral, or environmental indignities that communicate hostile, derogatory, or racial slights and insults toward people of color" (Sue et al., 2007, p. 271). Sue et al. (2007) further identify three critical forms of microaggressions: microassault, microinsult, and microinvalidation. The following chart provides definitions and examples of the critical forms of microaggressions.

MICROAGGRESSION EXAMPLES	
Microassault: Intentional explicit; overt racial attack (verbal or nonverbal)	✓ Being called "colored" ✓ Racist jokes ✓ Racial epithets ✓ Displaying a confederate flag
Microinsult: Subtle intentional or unintentional insulting message to the person of color	✓ Messages that communicate people of color are not qualified (references to affirmative action) ✓ "You are a credit to your race." ✓ Messages conveying that contributions from people of color are not valued ✓ "You are so articulate."

Microinvalidation: Communication that excludes the thoughts, feelings, or experiential reality of a person of color	✓ "I don't see color." ✓ "All lives matter." ✓ "I have Black friends." ✓ Nullifying the racial experience of people of color

Adapted from Sue et al. (2007).

Uprooting microaggressions is vital to the community because microaggressions are values and expressions of Whiteness that communicate racist messages to people of color. The equity work will not advance when members of the community are being harmed daily by being dismissed, invalidated, and insulted. The cumulative effect of microaggressions, over time, "can lead to frustration, self-doubt, and lower mental health" (Hopper, 2019, para. 12). The experience of being a victim of daily racial microaggressions is traumatic. Microaggressions have been described as a slow "death by a thousand cuts" (Torino, 2017, para. 5). One cut may not kill you, but a thousand cuts will impact your mental and physical health. Uprooting also refers to interrupting the people who perpetrate racial microaggressions unintentionally by building awareness of the impact of their actions.

Pause and Reflect

What racial microaggressions has Ms. Jackson experienced at True Elementary?

Co-Constructing Working Conditions That Facilitate Racial Equity Change

There is power in the prefix *co*. The prefix has three primary definitions (Merriam-Webster, 2020): "1. with: together: joint: jointly; 2. in or to the same degree; 3. one that is associated in action with another; fellow; partner." Establishing the working conditions in the environment *with* or *jointly* is an immediate investment in community building. Investment in the working conditions is an aspect of building a community.

- ✓ We **support** agency and autonomy.

- ✓ We are **accountable** to one another and commit to eliminating the alienation of our peers of color.

- ✓ We **uproot** racial microaggressions.

- ✓ We **co-construct** work conditions that facilitate racial equity change.

- ✓ We **elevate** teachers' humanity and racial identity.

SAUCE is not a linear process but a way to describe strategic considerations to assist the collective construction and application of conditions for building a transformative culture.

GOT SAUCE?

Supporting Agency and Autonomy

Agency and autonomy are interconnected; both are associated with a learner's (in this case, an educator's) willingness to engage in building their capacity. Agency is related to the learners' consciousness in initiating actions for a specific purpose, and autonomy is the educators' capacity to make decisions and take responsibility for their learning (Teng, 2019). In this context, the intended outcome is to make race-conscious decisions that change the outcomes for students of color. A component of the racial equity leader's role is to support the educator in being accountable for increasing their level of consciousness. However, the support does not cease at the point of increasing their level of consciousness; the application of their improved consciousness, in other words, putting it into action, is required to benefit the students they serve.

As a collective working toward transformative practices that center Black and Brown students, we follow a pathway that leads to racial equity change. Pathway in this context refers to a theory of change or a framework (in our case, the CARE framework) to ground the work. Another aspect of co-constructing working conditions is positive accountability, which aligns with the conditions we have agreed to. For example, if we jointly establish advocacy for Black children as one of our working conditions, our accountability includes calling out situations in which we failed to advocate for Black students.

Elevating Teachers' Humanity and Racial Identity

Educators' authenticity and how they display it in the environment should be embraced and understood. Embracing one's self-expression validates that person's humanity, especially if it is associated with their racial or cultural identity. As racial equity leaders, we must be especially aware of how our own biases color our perceptions of outward appearance (clothing, hair, piercings, tattoos, etc.) and how these biases can impact the way we interact with others. Your disposition will set the stage for how you show up in the space and how you elevate educators' humanity and racial identity. Educators showing up unapologetically to serve students are not the problem; rather, a culture that does not embrace and celebrate the power in how they show up is highly problematic.

Ideas to Sit With

Those of us who are in a position to hire teachers typically seek out candidates who appear to have some level of "spark" that we believe will help them engage their students. Educators show up to the interview as their best selves and land the opportunity. Yet, such decisions are never colorblind. Race inevitably has an impact on decision making. Schools may actively seek out candidates of color, or they may continue to perpetuate the practices that have limited the diversity of the team. Even when we take concrete actions to increase the diversity of our staffs, it seems that after the interview, something changes. "Just like students, teachers often are expected to leave 'who they are' at the door of the school. They are expected to be just a teacher, devoid of all the things that make them who they are" (Dixon et al., 2019, p. 16). Ask yourself: Why seek individuality, diversity, and voice only to allow it to be oppressed?

As the community begins to build momentum in applying their collective learning through the utilization of the CARE framework, it normalizes the application of an anti-oppression lens to demolish instructional and structural practices immersed in White supremacy.

According to Hardiman and Jackson (2007), oppression exists when the following four conditions are present:

1. The oppressor (person(s) with the power to determine) has the authority to dictate and define experiences (reality) for the members of the collective.

2. The oppressed (person(s) subjected to those determinations) internalize the negative messages and treatment from the oppressor and begin to take on the actions and behaviors of the oppressor.

3. Harassment, discrimination, exploitation, and marginalization are systemic and institutionalized and do not require conscious thought or effort to sustain the oppression.

4. Both the oppressed and oppressors are socialized to maintain their positions and the dominant culture continues to be imposed.

Journal Prompt

Given each of the four above-mentioned indicated conditions for oppression, how can an anti-oppression lens be applied to structural and institutional structures impacted by the conditions?

Strategies for Promoting and Pushing Growth From Discomfort to Dialogue

In previous chapters, you were introduced to the aspect of conflict and how it may appear in racial equity capacity building. As the racial equity leader and members of the team build community through establishing a culture that embraces trust and vulnerability, discomfort is expected. As the racial equity leader and a member of the community, you must promote and push growth to move from discomfort to dialogue to transformative actions.

The CARE framework provides sustenance to considering and creating conditions for educators to build their racial equity capacity. There will be opportunities to promote and push educators to continue growing toward their consciousness during the process. As you delve deeper into the examination of racism, Whiteness, and using a racial equity lens to examine structures, processes, and decision making, the discomfort will consistently surface. The framework also serves as a tool to help you navigate these waters. Acknowledge the discomfort but also uplift the need to engage through the discomfort to have the necessary dialogue. Even the highest performing, equity-centered environments experience discomfort and challenges. Yet, most educators will concur that discomfort and challenges can make substantial contributions to learning and growth. Being intentional in your approach to facilitating growth fosters a community that is not complacent in the face of practices that perpetuate adverse outcomes for students of color.

By now, it should be clear that part of being a racial equity leader is "having the educators' back." The attributes of our SAUCE acronym also support us in creating supportive environments that foster the professional growth needed to change the trajectory for students of color. Like classroom teachers, leaders must intentionally balance the natural tension between support and discomfort. This chapter sought to examine the importance of co-constructing conditions using an anti-oppression lens to engage in transformative practices that interrupt predictable patterns for students of color. From introspection (asking yourself questions such as What do I believe? Who am I? What role does my race play in my life?) to disrupting deeply rooted systemic structures, race equity work involves a willingness to question assumptions. Through questioning our assumptions about race, through the critical examination of institutions that disadvantage people of color, through honing our ability to honestly reflect on our personal, racial equity capacity, through furthering our readiness to value people of color (Williams & Reas, 2015), we embark on our equity journey. However, the "talking cure" is insufficient in reversing the predictable patterns that have harmed generations of students of color. No matter how committed we are to engage in personal and interpersonal work, if we neglect taking action (i.e., changing our policies, procedures, and practices), the systems of oppression will hold firm. The work can only be sustained when taken to the point where the inequities are challenged and we *take collective action* to unseat the structures that have oppressed students of color. Our collective engagement becomes the pathway to lasting change.

What Nobody Talks About

It is comfortable for a White person to exist in a racist society. Discomfort is necessary for interruption.

Your Lived Experience

As a leader engaging in racial equity work,

- In what ways will you model (among your sphere of influence) acting consciously to confront historic patterns of marginalization?

- How will you disrupt observable instances of oppression toward people of color through racism, sexism, homophobia, and all forms of discrimination?

Chapter Reflection

- What actions can a racial equity leader take to create accountability among the adults while disrupting conditions leading to the alienation of any member from the collective?

- How will you co-construct a supportive environment which disrupts ideas, structures, or practices that support White supremacy or concepts contrary to the fundamental goals of changing outcomes for students of color?

- As the racial equity leader, how will you emphasize the domains of personal, interpersonal, and structural within community building?

- The racial equity leader must navigate through people's discomfort to have necessary dialogue related to racial equity; how do you elevate teachers' humanity during the experience?

Final Thoughts 9

///

Throughout this book we have discussed intellectually, experientially, technically, and adaptively a process for negotiating and leading organizational transformation that dismantles structural racism and other forms of oppression. As we conclude this text, the trial of Derek Chauvin, the police officer who murdered George Floyd, recently concluded. There is a global pandemic that is showing few signs of abating. Although there is a vaccine that shows great promise for a return to "normal" life, there are reports from all over the country that show that the people most impacted by negative outcomes from contracting COVID-19 are the same groups who have the least amount of access to effective preventions like vaccines. Further, the Delta variant is lurking as an unknown. Notwithstanding this reality, most public school districts are preparing to open for fall 2021 with in-person learning with some parents of color most concerned about returning to in-person learning. It seems, in so many ways, that society is bursting at the seams trying to avoid the work of transformative change.

As we worked on this text, we had many more examples of early actions related to disrupting racial unconsciousness, co-constructing knowledge and ways of knowing, and applications of transformed holistic policies, practices, and procedures. We acknowledge the level of discourse on organizations that function fully using an anti-oppressionist lens is thin. We want to take an opportunity to both name this problem and explore our thoughts around causality.

Naming the Problem

1. **Anti-racist work is hard and requires ongoing vigilance.**

   Intersectional racial equity work requires different skills and energies than what we are most accustomed to expending. This is particularly true for those of you who occupy dominant identities. Surfacing trauma, discovering joy, naming miseducation, unpacking its impact, engaging different relationships with family, friends, colleagues, self, and so on all require a significant amount of emotional labor. Exhaustion is a risk. Self-care that rejuvenates the mind, body, and spirit and that keeps you hopeful and able to engage are not afterthoughts. Using structures like affinity groups, healing circles, listening sessions, and meditative practice are all techniques that we have found essential in both doing and sustaining this work. It is important that the challenge of this work is appropriately contextualized. Difficulty is not an indication that one is doing something wrong but that one is doing work that counts. Ensuring the culture supports transformed ways of being and engaging is essential.

2. **Systems of oppression are amazingly resilient.**

Identity advantaging and disadvantaging, valuing and de-valuing are normalized in American society. It is not an accident of history that Black people, Native/Indigenous people, Brown Hispanic people and other non-White people are to varying degrees, constantly fighting for inclusion. The systems that operate in society are built to advantage and serve the existing social order—the social order established at the inception of the American experiment and that did not include treating the previously named groups as full partners in the franchise. The definitions of race have changed over the period of American history. The mechanisms of marginalization and exclusion have changed over the period of American history. The level of violence (physical and structural) directed at non-White people has changed over history. These changes are not accidental; they are system adaptations to changes in culture. Systems of oppression favor culturally acceptable forms of expression. Culturally acceptable forms of expression typically exist within the bounds of a collective presumed "norm." It takes work to "see systems." It takes work and vigilance to prevent re-entrenchment. This work is never "done."

3. **Visioning undergirded by passion, commitment, and a plan is essential.**

   This work needs to be led with "why." What we do should be related to our foundational "why." How we do what we do should be emblematic of our "why." Personal work that centers individuals and collective in "why" is essential. It will be easier for organizations that haven't grounded their work in morality rooted injustice to drift back to old ways of being. Planning budgets, training plans, organizational growth, and so forth, are all intuitive professional responsibilities. Each year, we commit to these types of exercises, but the work of dismantling structural racism seems often to get very different treatment. A session here or there, a lack of support and accountability, and an inability to describe organizational development over time are characteristics that we have observed when there is no plan. This work can become toxic to employees who are the targets of structural inequity when there is no commitment for organizational change.

How We Can Create More Organizations That Operate Using an Anti-Oppressionist Lens

We named the problem and shared our thoughts on conditions that give roots and permanence to organizational inertia if these are not interrupted. Now we want to look forward. Specifically, what are those things that communities can habitually invest in, that tilt the balance in favor of anti-oppression as an organizational way of being? We understand that until more and more organizations create these conditions, they are aspirations . . . dreams, but we believe dreams are the stuff of new and different realities. So, dream with us, dream the dream of organizations' roots in the pursuit of justice, love in action. Here are our thoughts on essential conditions.

1. **Clearly communicate a vision of the possibilities (realized and yet to be realized) that describes a pluralist, multi-racial, multi-ethnic, gender-inclusive organization. This work is additive in quality.**

   Vision is essential to this work. What does an organization focused on and committed to just internal and external operations look like? How does it feel to be a part of this organization? How do staff serve the work of the organization? How does the organization serve its staff? The "perfect" is not the enemy of authentic engagement. We talk about organizations that engage in "performance," those that learn lessons through significant mistakes, and those that achieve significant improvements in an organization's health by de-centering Whiteness in its cultural singularity. There is no "one right way" to do this work. How is the team able to see, analyze, and describe the ways it is becoming more humanistic and inclusive? Are the voices of those most marginalized centered in this story telling? Do staff feel empowered to not only talk about the conditions in which they work but what it feels like to be in the transformed organizational culture? These are habits that organizations that are intolerant of unjust conditions adopt, internalize, and ultimately hire and spread around.

2. **Spend more time working with the staff on what you do want than what you don't.**

It is understandable why organizations focus dismantling dehumanizing practices when focused on intersectional race equity. From killing the body to killing the spirit, the damage dehumanization takes on an organization and its people is hard to find words to describe. We submit that while organizations are working on the work of dismantling, they must also focus on building a new reality. The same energy or greater energy on the organization's best most just self is a part of healing. This justice focus is a part of what will help persons harmed by the organization to find the energy they will need to remain connected to the institution. It is not enough to know that which causes pain but to be a part of that which creates joy and possibility is critical.

3. **Root this work centrally in the future viability of the organization.**

How does the internal work shape the external work? As you engage in healthy ways interpersonally, what does that mean for the external service or support you provide? What does that mean for your work with clients? Who does the organization become because of the transformation?

As we conclude this work, we would like the reader to grapple with both the difficulty and the simplicity. Change is hard, transformation is harder, but creating anti-racist organizations requires transformation, and change is an unacceptable substitute. The idea of transformation is that something must become different—in the multitude of ways an organization might need to negotiate difference. The simplicity proposition is to work within the collective to define the question of who you want to be internally in relationship with one another, stay committed to that vision, and be open to how it defines the organizational character anew.

We are in a moment when the impacts of the coronavirus pandemic and racial terror are colliding to make daily life challenging at best, overwhelming on average. In 2021, equity, anti-racism, and racial equity work is everywhere. It is in places and on the lips of the thoughtful and the thoughtless. It is proffered in educational organizations, NFL, NBA, Olympic Committee non-profits, religious institutions, government agencies, and this list can go on and on. The authors want to leave the readers with these ideas as the work of anti-racism (with all its potential intersections) is the work of humanizing spaces. Without commitment to the difficult process involved in de-institutionalizing oppression, that more harm can be caused is almost a certainty. Given this admonition, we invite the readers of this text to deeply consider the thoughts offered herein. Those trusting your leadership need you to be worthy of said trust.

References

Chapter 1: Race Matters Because Racism Does

Alexander, M. (2010). *The new Jim Crow: Mass incarceration in the age of colorblindness*. New York, NY: New Press.

Anderson, C. (2016). *White rage: The unspoken truth*. New York, NY: Bloomsbury.

Annie E. Casey Foundation. (2014). *Early reading proficiency and young men of color*. http://gradelevelreading.net/wp-content/uploads/2014/02/GLR-white-house-charts-1pg-r6.pdf

Aud, S., Fox, M., & KewalRamani, A. (2010). *Status and trends in the education of racial and ethnic groups*. Washington, DC: National Center for Education Statistics.

Carson, E. A. (2015). *Prisoners in 2014*. Washington, DC: Bureau of Justice Statistics.

CBS News. (2020, January 9). Teacher accused of making racist slideshow. https://www.cbsnews.com/video/teacher-accused-of-making-racist-slideshow/

Chetty, R., Hendren, N., Jones, M., and Porter, S. (2020). Race and economic opportunity in the United States: An intergenerational perspective. *Quarterly Journal of Economics, 135*(2), 711–783.

Coulson, D. (2015). British Imperialism, the Indian Independence Movement, and the racial eligibility provisions of the Naturalization Act: *United States v. Thind* revisited. *Georgetown Journal of Law & Modern Critical Race Perspectives, 7*(2015): 1–42.

Dailymail.com. (2019, December 22). Teacher who allegedly said she wanted to "bring back slavery" to young students is placed on leave. https://www.dailymail.co.uk/news/article-7816893/Teacher-allegedly-said-wanted-bring-slavery-young-students-placed-leave.html

Dates, J. (1980). Race, racial attitudes and adolescent perceptions of Black television characters. *Journal of Broadcasting, 24*(4), 549–560.

Defender News Service. (2019, November 19). Teachers under fire for racist text chain. https://defendernetwork.com/news/national/teachers-under-fire-for-racist-text-chain/

Dixon, T. (2007). Black criminals and White officers: The effects of racially misrepresenting lawbreakers and law defenders on television news. *Media Psychology, 10*, 270–291.

Dixon, T. (2017). A dangerous distortion of our families: Representation of families by race in news and opinion media. https://colorofchange.org/dangerousdistortion/

Donaldson, L. (2015, August 12). When the media misrepresents Black men, the effects are felt in the real world. *The Guardian.* https://www.theguardian.com/commentisfree/2015/aug/12/media-misrepresents-black-men-effects-felt-real-world

González, J., & Torres, J. (2011). *News for all the people: The epic story of race and the American media.* London, UK: Verso.

Guyatt, N. (2016). *Bind us apart: How enlightened Americans invented racial segregation.* New York, NY. Basic Books.

Hannah-Jones, N., Elliott, M., Hughes, J., & Silverstein, J. (2019, August 18). The 1619 project. *New York Times Magazine.*

Happer, C., & Philo, G. (2013). The role of the media in the construction of public belief and social change. *Journal of Social and Political Psychology, 1*(1), 321–336. doi:10.5964/jspp.v1i1.96

Hayes, C. (2018, August 14, 2020). Here are 10 times President Trump's comments have been called racist. *USA Today.* https://www.usatoday.com/story/news/politics/onpolitics/2018/08/14/times-president-trump-comments-called-racist/985438002/

Heifetz, R. A., Linsky, M., & Grashow, A. (2009). *The practice of adaptive leadership.* Boston, MA: Harvard Business Review Press.

Jefferson, T. (1774). *Declaration of Independence.* Jefferson Paper: Library of Congress. https://www.loc.gov/item/mtjbib000159/

Klarman, M. (2004). *From Jim Crow to civil rights: The Supreme Court and the struggle for racial equity.* Oxford, UK: Oxford University Press.

Luther, C., Lepre, C. R., & Clark, N. (2012). *Diversity in U.S. mass media.* Malden, MA: Wiley Blackwell.

Malcolm X. (n.d.). Influence quotes. https://www.brainyquote.com/topics/influence-quotes

Mastro, D. (2017, September 26). Race and ethnicity in US media content and effects. In *Oxford Research Encyclopedia of Communication.* Oxford, UK: Oxford University Press. https://oxfordre.com/communication/view/10.1093/acrefore/9780190228613.001.0001/acrefore-9780190228613-e-122

Mastro, D. E., & Kopacz, M. A. (2006). Media representations of race, proto-typicality, and policy reasoning: An application of self-categorization theory. *Journal of Broadcasting & Electronic Media, 50*(2), 305–322.

Neill, K. A., Yusuf, J., & Morris, J. C. (2014). Explaining dimensions of state-level punitiveness in the United States: The roles of social, economic, and cultural factors. *Criminal Justice Policy Review, 26*(2), 751–772.

Opportunity Agenda. (2011). *Media representations and impact on the lives of Black men and boys: Media portrayals and Black male outcomes.* https://www.opportunityagenda.org/explore/resources-publications/media-representations-impact-black-men/media-portrayals

Painter, N. I. (2010). *The history of White people.* New York, NY: Norton.

Peffley, M., Shields, T., & Williams, B. (1996). The intersection of race and crime in television news stories: An experimental study. *Political Communication, 13*(3), 309–327. https://doi.org/10.1080/10584609.1996.9963120

Rothenstein, R. (2004). *Class and schools: Using social, economic, and educational reform to close the Black-White achievement gap.* Washington, DC: Economic Policy Institute.

Shea, D. (2017, December 7). Uncovered: Possible inspiration for controversial LeBron James *Vogue* cover. *Huffington Post.* https://www.huffpost.com/entry/uncovered-possible-inspir_n_93944

Tan, A., Fujioka, Y., & Tan, G. (2000). Television use, stereotypes of African Americans and opinions on affirmative action: An affective model of policy reasoning. *Communication Monographs, 67*(4), 362–371.

Taylor, A., & Foner, E. (2002). *American colonies: The settling of North America.* New York, NY: Penguin Books.

Torres, J. (2018, March 7). Racism in the media persists 50 years after Kerner report. *Free Press.* www.freepress.net/our-response/expert-analysis/insights-opinions/racism-media-persists-50-years-after-kerner-report

Wilkerson, I. (2020). *Caste: The origins of our discontents.* New York, NY: Random House.

Woodson, C. G. (1933). *The mis-education of the Negro.* Washington, DC: Associated Publishers.

Chapter 2: Building Community by Reimagining New Possibilities

Brown, B. (2012). *Daring greatly: How the courage to be vulnerable transforms the way we live, love, parent, and lead.* New York, NY: Avery.

Greenia, A. (2018, November 2). The role of White co-conspirators in dismantling systemic racism. *Embracing Equity.* https://embracingequity.org/blog/2018/11/2/let-us-work-together-the-role-of-white-co-conspirators-in-dismantling-systemic-racism

Jordan, C., Orozco, E., & Averret, A. (2001). *Emerging issues in school, family, & community connections*. Austin, TX: Southwest Educational Development Laboratory.

Parent Involvement in Public Education: A Literature Review May 2008 Cecily Mitchell – Research for Action 701 Chestnut Street • Philadelphia, PA

King, M. L., Jr. (1966, May 4). *Nonviolence: The only road to freedom*. Gilder Lehrman Institute of American History. https://www.gilderlehrman.org/sites/default/files/inline-pdfs/mlk_nonviolence_abridged.pdf

Chapter 3: Confronting Blame by Reframing Accountability

Aguilar, E. (2016, March 22). *Managing conflict in school leadership teams*. Edutopia. https://www.edutopia.org/blog/managing-conflict-school-leadership-teams-elena-aguilar

Brown, B. (2012). *Daring greatly: How the courage to be vulnerable transforms the way we live, love, parent, and lead*. New York, NY: Avery.

Brown, B. (2015). The anatomy of trust [Video podcast episode]. *Super Soul Sessions*. https://brenebrown.com/videos/anatomy-trust-video/

DiAngelo, R. (2011). White fragility. *The International Journal of Critical Pedagogy, 3*(3), 54–70.

Dinsmore, P. C. (1988). Proactive conflict management. *Project Management Journal, 19*(1), 15–16.

Galloway, M., & Ishimaru, A. (2019). Leading equity teams: The role of formal leaders in building organizational capacity for equity. *Journal of Education for Students Placed at Risk (JESPAR), 25*(2), 107–125. https://doi.org/10.1080/10824669.2019.1699413

Henry, T. (2020). *Toxic: Dealing with a culture of blame*. Accidental Creative. https://accidentalcreative.com/teams/toxic-dealing-with-a-culture-of-blame/

Hewson, M. (2010). Agency. In A. J. Mills, G. Durepos, & E. Wiebe (Eds.), *Encyclopedia of case study research* (pp. 13–16). Thousand Oaks, CA: SAGE. doi:10.4135/9781412957397.n5

Lencioni, P. (2002). *The five dysfunctions of a team*. San Francisco, CA: Jossey-Bass.

Lorde, A. (1984). *Sister outsider: Essays and speeches*. Trumansburg, NY: Crossing Press.

Martin, J. (2020, September 22). Donald Trump announces ban on "sex and race-based ideologies" extends to companies with government contracts. *Newsweek*. https://www.newsweek.com/donald-trump-announces-ban-sex-race-based-ideologies-extends-companies-government-contracts-1533714

Modoono, J. (2017). The trust factor. *Education Leadership, 74*(8). http://www.ascd.org/publications/educational-leadership/may17/vol74/num08/The-Trust-Factor.aspx

Morrison, B., & Vaandering, D. (2012). Restorative justice: Pedagogy, praxis, and discipline. *Journal of School Violence, 11*(2), 138–155.

Russell, N. S. (2016). 15 communication mistakes that can diminish trust. *Psychology Today.* https://www.psychologytoday.com/us/blog/trust-the-new-workplace-currency/201604/15-communication-mistakes-can-diminish-trust

Saphier, J. (2018). Let's get specific about how leaders can build trust. *The Learning Professional, 39*(6). https://learningforward.org/journal/december-2018-volume-39-no-6/lets-get-specific-about-how-leaders-can-build-trust/

Chapter 4: Power and Influence

Crenshaw, K. (2017, June 8). *Kimberlé Crenshaw on intersectionality, more than two decades later.* Columbia Law School. https://www.law.columbia.edu/news/archive/kimberle-crenshaw-intersectionality-more-two-decades-later

Lawrence, K., & Keleher, T. (2004). *Chronic disparity: Strong and pervasive evidence of racial inequalities; Poverty outcomes; Structural racism.* https://www.intergroupresources.com/rc/Definitions%20of%20Racism.pdf

Chapter 5: Invisibility and Other Barriers to Engaging in the Work of Anti-Racism Structural Transformation

Costello, M., & Dillard, C. (2019). *Hate at school* (Special Report). Montgomery, AL: Southern Poverty Law Center. https://www.splcenter.org/sites/default/files/tt_2019_hate_at_school_report_final_0.pdf

Ellison, R. (1995). *Invisible man.* New York, NY: Vintage International.

Merriam-Webster. (n.d.). Marginalize. *Merriam-Webster.com dictionary.* https://www.merriam-webster.com/dictionary/marginalize

Chapter 6: Creating Space for Productive Struggle

Collins, P. (2012). *On intellectual activism.* Philadelphia, PA: Temple University Press.

Fong-Olivares, Y. (2018, May 17). Addressing racial equity with an organizational change lens. *Philanthropy News Digest.* https://philanthropynewsdigest.org/commentary-and-opinion/addressing-racial-equity-with-an-organizational-change-lens

Hecht, B. (2020, June 16). Moving beyond diversity toward racial equity. *Harvard Business Review.* https://hbr.org/2020/06/moving-beyond-diversity-toward-racial-equity

Heifetz, R. A., Linsky, M., & Grashow, A. (2009). *The practice of adaptive leadership.* Boston, MA: Harvard Business Review Press.

Jones, K., & Okun, T. (2001). The characteristics of White supremacy culture. Change Work. https://www.showingupforracialjustice.org/white-supremacy-culture-characteristics.html

Livingston, R. (2020, September–October). How to promote racial equity in the workplace. *Harvard Business Review*. https://hbr.org/2020/09/how-to-promote-racial-equity-in-the-workplace

Powell, J. A. (2008). Structural racism: Building upon the insights of John Calmore. *North Carolina Law Review, 86*, 791–816.

Singleton, G. (2015). *Courageous conversations about race* (2nd ed.). Thousand Oaks, CA: Corwin.

Chapter 7: Application of Equity Lens for System Change

Au, W. (2019, Summer). White supremacy, high-stakes testing, and the punishment of Black and Brown students. *Rethinking Schools, 33*(4). https://rethinkingschools.org/articles/racial-justice-is-not-a-choice/

Hammond, Z. (2015). *Culturally responsive teaching and the brain: Promoting authentic engagement and rigor among culturally and linguistically diverse students*. Thousand Oaks, CA: Corwin.

Hunt Institute. (n.d.). *Evolution of the Elementary and Secondary Education Act, 1965 to 2015*. http://www.hunt-institute.org/wp-content/uploads/2016/09/Development-of-the-Elementary-and-Secondary-Education-Act-August-2016.pdf

National Assessment of Educational Progress. (2020). *The Nation's Report Card: Results from the 2019 Mathematics and Reading Assessments*. https://www.nationsreportcard.gov/mathematics/supportive_files/2019_infographic.pdf

National Center for Education Statistics. (2014). *The Nation's Report Card: Mathematics and Reading 2013: Trends in 4th- and 8th-grade NAEP mathematics and reading average scores and score gaps, by NSLP eligibility*. Washington, DC: U.S. Department of Education, Institute of Education Sciences.

Race Forward. (2006, April 13). *Historical timeline of public education in the US*. https://www.raceforward.org/research/reports/historical-timeline-public-education-us

University of Minnesota, University Policy Library. (n.d.). Equity lens. Retrieved September 25, 2020 from https://policy.umn.edu/equity-lens/

Chapter 8: Building to Transformation Through Collective Application

Battey, D., & Leyva, L. A. (2016). A framework for understanding Whiteness in mathematics education. *Journal of Urban Mathematics Education, 9*(2). https://doi.org/10.21423/jume-v9i2a294

Brewley-Kennedy, D. (2005). The struggles of incorporating equity into practice in a university mathematics methods course. *Mathematics Educator*. Monograph 1. 16–28.

Costa, A., & Kallick, B. (1993). Through the lens of a critical friend. *New Roles, New Relationships*, 51(2), 49–51.

DiAngelo, R. (2011). White fragility. *International Journal of Critical Pedagogy*, *3*(3), 54–70.

Dixon, D., Griffin, A. & Teoh, M. (2019, September). *If you listen, we will stay.* The Education Trust/Teacher Plus. https://files.eric.ed.gov/fulltext/ED603193.pdf

Hardiman, R., Jackson, B., & Griffin, P. (2007). *Conceptual foundations for social justice education.* In M. Adams, L. A. Bell, & P. Griffin (Eds.), *Teaching for diversity and social justice* (p. 35–66). New York, NY: Routledge.

Hopper, E. (2019, July 3). What is a microaggression? Everyday insults with harmful effects. ThoughtCo. https://www.thoughtco.com/microaggression-definition-examples-4171853

Merriam-Webster. (n.d.). *Co-* prefix. *Merriam-Webster.com dictionary.* Retrieved August 16, 2020, from https://www.merriam-webster.com/dictionary/co-

Milner, H. (2020) Black teacher: White school. *Theory Into Practice, 59*(4), 400–408. https://doi.org/10.1080/00405841.2020.1773180

Sue, D., Capodilupo, C., Torino, G., Bucceri, J., Holder, A., Nadal, K., & Esquilin, M. (2007). Racial microaggressions in everyday life: Implications for clinical practice. *American Psychologist.* 62(4), 271–286. https://www.cpedv.org/sites/main/files/file-attachments/how_to_be_an_effective_ally-lessons_learned_microaggressions.pdf

Teng, M. (2019, November 10). Understanding teacher autonomy, teacher agency, and teacher identity: Voices from four EFL student teachers. *English Teaching & Learning, 43*, 189–212. https://link.springer.com/article/10.1007%2Fs42321-019-00024-3

Torino, G. (2017). *How racism and microaggressions lead to worse health.* Center for Health Journalism. https://www.centerforhealthjournalism.org/2017/11/08/how-racism-and-microaggressions-lead-worse-health

Williams, H., & Reas, R. (2015). An introspection on race, ethnicity, and national origin. *National Forum of Multicultural Issues Journal, 12*(1).

INDEX

Accountability, 27, 30, 31, 36,
    38, 58, 64, 78, 79, 102, 116,
    118, 120, 127
Active engagement, 40–41
Active listening, 41, 51
Adult learning, 29, 31, 66
Aguilar, E., 49
Alexander, M., 16
Alienation, 118, 120
Anti-oppression, 3, 31, 58, 59,
    63, 68, 90, 116, 121, 123,
    125, 127–129
Anti-racism, 3, 27, 28, 31, 59,
    61–63, 66, 81, 92, 93, 129
Anti-racist
    leadership, 29, 58
    organization, 27, 28, 30, 31,
        67–68, 129
    work, 3, 64, 82, 88, 125–126
Authenticity, 66, 121
    engagement, 42, 65, 88, 89, 128
    relationships, 37, 39, 59, 102
Awareness, 19, 31, 48, 49, 74–75,
    90, 92, 93, 118, 119

Baldwin, J., 18, 31, 94, 95, 98
Battey, D., 115
Black Codes, 15, 16
Black families, 22
Black gorilla, 20, 21
Black Lives Matter, 35, 41, 55, 56, 61
Blackness, 12, 20, 57, 82
Black Parents Action Group, 65

Blame, 37–39, 49, 90, 91
Brown, B., 30, 39
*Brown v. Board of Education of
    Topeka*, 15, 17, 100

Capacity building, 1, 27, 92, 93, 122
Caste (Wilkerson), 75
Co-constructing knowledge, 31,
    49, 59, 68, 90, 105, 116, 117,
    119–120, 123, 125
Collective agency, 38
Collective responsibility, 30–32, 60
College and Career Readiness
    Standards, 100–101
Collins, P., 94
Colorblindness, 75, 83
Communication, 49, 51, 79, 107, 108
Community
    beloved, 26, 28, 29, 36, 60, 63, 77
    building, 27–30, 36–38, 45, 48,
        51, 59, 119, 121–122
    marginalization in, 79
    microaggressions to, 119
    radical, 78
    vision of, 28
Conflict
    address the, 49
    anchor team members, 49
    anticipating, 94–95
    fear of open, 91
    healthy, 47, 48, 81
    name the, 49
    unhealthy, 47–50

Conscious and anti-racist
    engendering (CARE)
    framework, 23, 27–31, 38,
    43, 45, 48, 49, 58–61, 73, 90,
    91, 93, 99, 102, 105–106, 116,
    117, 121–123
Council of Chief State School
    Officers (CCSSO), 101
COVID-19, 36, 98
*Cowan and United States v. Bolivar
    County Board of Education
    No. 4.*, 100
Crenshaw, K., 56
Cultural
    competence, 78–79
    invisibility, 82–83
Curiosity, 82–83
Curriculum, 18, 61–63, 107
    Eurocentric, 62, 66, 98,
        99, 101, 110
    national, 101

Data-informed process, 68
Decision making, 43, 76, 77, 92,
    103, 105–107, 109, 121, 122
Declaration of Independence, 14
DiAngelo, R., 46, 115, 134
Discipline practices, 107–108
Disconnection, 50–51
Dixon, T., 22
Donaldson, L., 22
Drew Scott v. John F. Sandford, 15

Elementary and Secondary
    Education Act
    (ESEA), 101, 102
Ellison, R., 82
Equity, 3, 37–39, 46, 47, 49–51, 58,
    59, 67, 68, 80, 88, 94, 99–106,
    119, 123, 125, 129
Exchanging in professional
    conversations, 40, 41
Expertise-based power, 64–65

Fong-Olivares, Y., 93
Friendliness, 80

Guyatt, N., 13

Hammond, Z., 99
Hardiman, R., 121
Hewson, M., 38
Hiring practices, 108
Home-school connection, 108
Honor, 2, 16, 29, 40, 59, 77, 90,
    94, 104, 107
Human-centered accountability, 78
Humanity, 1–3, 5, 6, 13, 59, 62,
    77–79, 90, 95, 116, 121–122

Identity
    interpersonal, 74–75
    personal identity
        development, 74–77
    racial, 29–31, 78, 121–122
Individualism, 59–61
Instructional resources, 108–109
Intentionality, 82
Interruptions, 32, 44–46, 50, 57,
    67, 81, 83, 93, 104, 110, 115
Intersectionality, 56, 93
Intersectional racial equity, 3–5, 59,
    79, 107, 125–126
Investment, 76, 88, 93, 102, 110, 119
Invisible Man (Ellison), 82

Jackson, B., 121
James, L., 20
Jim Crow laws, 15, 16

Kindergarten, 9–13, 65
King, M. L. Jr., 26, 28, 29, 60

Lencioni, P., 46
Leyva, L. A., 115

Malcolm X, 21
Marginalization, 1, 3, 4, 17, 21, 28,
    30, 36, 43, 59, 67, 74, 79, 80,
    82, 98–100, 103, 105–107,
    122, 126, 128
Media, 18–23
Merriam-Webster. (n.d.), 79

Microaggressions, 60, 118–119
Milliken v. Bradley, 100
Modern-day schooling, 100–103
Morrison, B., 50

Nationalization Act of 1790, 14
New Jim Crow, The
        (Alexander), 16
Niceness, 80, 81
No Child Left Behind
        (NCLB), 101–103

Obama, B., 13, 101
Organizational
    construction, 76
    culture, 55, 59, 60, 89, 128
    norms, 89
    performative wokeness, 63
    transformation, 1, 27, 31, 60, 125
Organization Effectiveness
        Plan, 26

Painter, N. I., 13
Plessy v. Ferguson, 15, 100
Positional power, 63–64
Power, 56–62
    and authority, 28
    and influence, 63–65
    interrogate, 94
    nature of, 68
    positional, 26, 28
    and privilege, 31
    in racial equity, 62–63
    and status, 50
    types of, 63–65
Proactive, 47–50
Productive struggle,
        92–95, 99–100
Professional conversation, 41
Professional development, 109
Public education system, 16–18

Qualitative data, 26, 28, 29, 89,
        99, 103–106
Quantitative data, 26, 28, 29, 88,
        89, 99, 103–106

Questions to Reengage in
        Conversation, 44–46, 51

Race
    equity lens, 76
    invisibility, 18
    in media, 18–23
    in public education, 16–18
Racial
    capacity, 92, 116
    consciousness, 37, 59, 94, 106
    diversity, 57
    equity, 4, 5, 38–41, 43, 45–48,
        50, 51, 57, 61–63, 66, 67, 76,
        79–82, 89, 92, 99, 105, 107,
        115–123, 125
    expression, 76–77
    harassment, 74
    identity, 29–31, 78, 121–122
    inequity, 37, 44, 62, 98
    microaggressions, 118–119
    stamina, 82
Racism, 23, 30
    anti-racism, 3, 27, 28, 31,
        59, 61–63, 66, 81,
        92, 93, 129
    institutional, 3, 14–16, 29, 57,
        58, 66, 81
    in media, 18–23
    structural, 36, 58, 61, 63, 64, 73,
        89, 92, 125, 127
    systemic, 4, 16–18, 50, 57, 102
Reactive, 47–51
Relational power, 64, 78
Restoration, 47, 50–51
Right to comfort, 91

Scheduling, 107, 109
School Improvement Plans, 26
Self-examination, 30, 94
Singleton, G., 94
Social arrangement, 57–59
Socialization, 16, 17, 66, 80
Social justice, 4, 36
Social media, 36
Southern Poverty Law Center, 74

Strategic lens of engagement, 59
Strategic planning, 28, 59, 68
Structural inequality, 4, 58, 59,
        88–90, 127
Student engagement, 107, 109
Sue, D., 118
Support, accountable, uproot,
        co-construct, elevate (SAUCE),
        117, 120, 123
Supportive environment,
        116–117, 123
Systems of oppression, 4, 16, 21, 23,
        57, 59, 62–64, 75, 78, 80, 94,
        98–100, 115, 123, 126

Tatum, B., 30
Technical solution, 15, 16,
        68, 101, 102
Thirteenth Amendment, 15, 16
Transformative process, 103–110
Trump, D., 36

Trust, 30, 31, 37–48, 93, 122, 129
Trust building, 39, 43–45

Vaandering, D., 50
Vogue, 20–21
Vulnerability, 30, 37–39, 43–45

White fragility (DiAngelo),
        46–47, 115
Whiteness
    de-centering, 61, 99, 128
    norms of, 116, 117
    socialization of, 17
White privilege, 36, 46
White racial hegemony, 75, 76, 82
White supremacy culture/White
        dominant culture, 4–5, 16, 19,
        20, 22, 26–27, 29, 30, 36, 43,
        46, 93, 110, 115, 116, 121
Wilkerson, I., 13, 75
Woodson, C. G., 17

A SAGE Publishing Company

Helping educators make the greatest impact

CORWIN HAS ONE MISSION: to enhance education through intentional professional learning.

We build long-term relationships with our authors, educators, clients, and associations who partner with us to develop and continuously improve the best evidence-based practices that establish and support lifelong learning.